Mentoring Teachers in Post Compulsory Education

Also available:

In at the Deep End
A survival guide for teachers in post compulsory education
Jim Crawley
1-84312-253-7

Leadership in Post Compulsory Education
Inspiring leaders of the future
Jill Jameson
1-84312-339-8

Teaching 14–19
Everything you need to know about learning and teaching across the phases
Gina Donovan
1-84312-342-8

Teaching in Post Compulsory Education
Policy, practice and values
Anthony Coles
1-84312-233-2

Teaching Business Education 14–19
Martin Jephcote and Ian Abbott
1-84312-254-5

Mentoring Teachers in Post Compulsory Education

A Guide to Effective Practice

Bryan Cunningham

 David Fulton Publishers

David Fulton Publishers Ltd
The Chiswick Centre, 414 Chiswick High Road, London W4 5TF

www.fultonpublishers.co.uk

David Fulton Publishers is a division of Granada Learning, part of ITV plc.

First published in Great Britain in 2005 by David Fulton Publishers.

10 9 8 7 6 5 4 3 2 1

Copyright © Bryan Cunningham 2005

British Library Cataloguing in Publication Data
A catalogue record for this book is available from the British Library.

ISBN 1-84312-316-9

Typeset by Servis Filmsetting Ltd, Manchester

Printed and bound in Great Britain

Contents

Acknowledgements

First and foremost I would like to acknowledge all the contributions made to my understanding of mentoring processes by the hundreds of trainees with whom I have worked over the years at the Institute of Education. Many of them have shared their viewpoints with me, as have a number of those trainees who have followed the PGCE/CertEd courses offered by Cardiff University, for which I acted as External Examiner from 2001 to 2005. There are too many such individuals to name, and some would, in any event, wish to retain their anonymity. Some especially important insights which *can* be attributed, however, were those of Juliet Harrison and Jo Shah.

The valuable conversations with John Parnell and his team at Cardiff have also played a part in shaping my ideas. So, too, of course, have been the myriad exchanges I have had with those practising mentors who have supported my trainees. The best mentoring I have encountered among them represents the very highest standards of professionalism. Steve Poland, Director of Human Resources at Tower Hamlets College, kindly read and commented in detail on the concluding chapter. Norman Lucas at the Institute of Education, and Patricia King at Standards Verification UK offered helpful advice and updating regarding the recent shifts in the policy environment in which teacher training takes place. My correspondence and conversations with Amanda Davidson at West Kent College were also of much value. Sarah Moore and Caroline Steenman-Clark assisted me tolerantly in my continuing struggle to understand both what goes on inside my computer and something of the logic of typography. Tracey Alcock of David Fulton Publishers waited patiently for the results.

Introduction

This guide has been produced as an attempt to collate and review the key dimensions of mentoring as a professional activity in colleges. It draws on the writer's own experiences as a teacher, mentor and teacher trainer, and on a range of texts and documents which practising mentors may not have the time, or inclination, to read in full. Far more importantly, however, the content and focus of the guide have been shaped by the actual experiences and views of the large number of mentors and trainees who have shared these with me over the past 15 or so years. If it is still at all appropriate to write in terms of a 'theory–practice divide' in education, it is strongly hoped that this contribution to effective mentoring is viewed as falling on the practical side of that divide.

Where I draw on selected theoretical perspectives I do so for the important reason that they appear to offer credible, helpful insights to complement a 'good sense' view of mentoring. It is hoped, on the one hand, that the avoidance of an in-depth examination of theories of professional learning and of mentoring will not be judged to have resulted in too superficial an approach. On the other hand, I am well aware of the possible risks attached to the inclusion in any 'guide to effective practice' of even abbreviated versions of significant theories; but their inclusion is probably symptomatic of the risks run by 'academics' when addressing practitioners working in very demanding educational settings.

Mentoring does not take place in a vacuum, and for this reason the guide also attempts to contextualise the activity by reviewing certain relevant socio-political and organisational developments. There is much that is taking place outside of post-compulsory education that can usefully inform our efforts to establish mentoring as a core activity in colleges.

In setting out the kinds of ideas most deserving of inclusion in a relatively short guide, the aim was to include those that were felt to be of particular value to a readership including not only practising mentors but also individuals in such other groups as:

- teacher trainers, perhaps most especially those fairly new to this role;
- staff developers in colleges;
- human resources managers in colleges;
- college teachers aspiring to take on mentoring responsibilities, possibly alongside such other related designations as 'beacons' or 'advanced skills' practitioners; and
- trainee teachers themselves, a quite surprising number of whom have in the past posed the question 'Yes, but what *exactly* is my mentor supposed to be doing?'

Certain groups in the above list, particularly those with management responsibilities in colleges, will be concerned not just with the interpersonal aspects of mentoring but also with broader, strategic and institutional affairs. For this reason I have devoted a section of Chapter 1 to what I have called the essential *architecture* of mentoring. The term is meant to denote those 'design features' of an institution that are strongly conducive to the activity.

What I would very much hope emerges from a reading of this guide is that its concern is not to present a rigid orthodoxy, or dogma, of mentoring practice. It is indeed possible to propose certain guidelines that can inform good practice, but fundamentally mentoring is a professional transaction that can assume an almost infinite variety of forms. The 'contours' of the transaction, and of the relationship as a whole, will be moulded by the experience, educational philosophy, attitudes and personal style of both of the principal actors – mentor and trainee. Eliot Freidson (2001) argues convincingly that professional activity cannot be standardised – that one of its defining characteristics is the way in which specialist knowledge is applied *with discretion*. If we accept this position, then logically we must acknowledge that no two mentors will, or should, operate in precisely the same way. However, by offering here certain important perspectives on mentoring it is hoped that a fuller range of potentially useful strategies can be drawn on than might be possible purely on the basis of intuition. My main aims were, then, to avoid dogmatism, and to examine the *why* as well as the *how* of mentoring, and in so doing stimulate a deeper reflective process focusing on the scope, purposes and limitations of the activity.

The changing policy environment

I am aware that, as with probably the majority of books being written at any one time on matters relating to education and training in the UK, the risk of including material that is likely to be dated by the time of publication is high.

At the time of writing, the nature and scope of the OfSTED/ALI college inspection process seems far from fixed. The Further Education National Training Organisation (FENTO) has just (January 2005) evolved into Standards Verification UK (SVUK) and the professional standards set by this body will, imminently – i.e. for publication by the middle of 2006 – be revised in a major way. Lifelong Learning UK (LLUK), as the relevant Sector Skills Council, looks set to play an important part in shaping post-compulsory education and training; and there are great hopes being expressed for the ability of the Institute for Learning (IfL) to aid in the professionalisation project sought for the sector.

Changes are afoot in the range of qualifications available to college learners, even though the reforms proposed by the recent 14–19 White Paper (DfES 2005) will not be entirely finalised for some time, and will probably take a decade or so to implement. Although the changes which the government will endorse are not likely to be as radical as those proposed by the Tomlinson Committee, they are still of great significance. This last consideration is highly relevant simply because it is not, therefore, at all straightforward to write confidently about the 'essential knowledge' regarding the post-14 curriculum which mentors should possess as they induct trainees into the PCET sector.

Furthermore, there are continuing discussions within policy and academic circles concerning the present lack of parity between qualifications for teaching at the respective levels of the UK education system, which may ultimately result in changes coming about, and the introduction – extremely belatedly – of Qualified Teacher Status for new entrants to college teaching. The most up-to-date perspective on this issue seems to point to the award of QTLS (Qualified Teacher Learning and Skills) following successful completion of a two-stage training process comprising 'passport to teaching' and 'full' programmes (DfES 2004: 4), shown diagrammatically as Appendix 1. In due course, this award could well be given under the auspices of the Institute for Learning referred to above (although only recently this was still being described as 'a body for college teachers that has yet to attract many members' (Kingston 2004)).

The key DfES document 'Equipping our Teachers for the Future' can provide a fuller review of some of the likely changes mentioned here and will also serve to draw strong attention to the much greater prominence that mentoring looks like having within the new scheme of things:

> Subject-specific skills must be acquired in the teachers' workplace and from vocational or academic experience. Mentoring, either by line managers, subject experts or experienced teachers in related curriculum areas, *is essential*.
>
> (DfES 2004: 8, emphasis added)

This is a radical statement of intent, as any kind of residual notion we might have that mentoring can be seen as an 'optional extra' in the training of new teachers is removed from our thinking.

Rationale for, and scope of, the book

The rationale for producing this guide is, first, that mentoring has become an altogether more prominent dimension of training for college teaching than it was until very recently. The value of *subject-specific mentoring* in particular is becoming a major preoccupation of policy-makers and academics. The complexities and demands of college teaching have never been greater, and to most confidently deal with these as a trainee it is contended that a mentor's guidance, beginning at the induction stage, is of great value, and even, many would say, essential.

Mentoring, like teaching itself, is viewed in this guide as having at its core a 'trainable' set of skills, rather than being based purely on an innate disposition to help and nurture – such human qualities are highly desirable ones in a mentor, but in isolation from professional and practical knowledge and experience, and concrete ways to give trainees the benefit of these, their value is greatly lessened. The guide therefore attempts to *link* mentors' professionalism and positive personal attributes with the many ways in which these can be actively deployed in the support of trainees in colleges.

The guide is designed to *structure and support* the work that mentors will be undertaking with teachers on their training programmes, either pre- or in-service. There are, of course, some major differences between these two types of courses, but there are also many similarities. For example, a trainee on a part-time, in-service CertEd or PGCE course, who has been newly appointed to a college's staff, may well experience as many uncertainties, and may be as disorientated by the newness of life as a college teacher, as a recent graduate moving straight from university to a full-time one-year programme and only attending a 'placement' college for their teaching practice.

A new appointee will sometimes find they have almost as lowly a status as a 'student' teacher in terms of, for example, being able to influence departmental policies and practices. Longer-serving, but previously untrained, college teachers may, on the other hand, experience special difficulties attached to finding themselves 'on the other side of the desk' for those parts of the week when they are attending their training programme. While many feel positive – excited even – about having been given the chance to formally qualify as teachers, others may feel a sense of grievance that their existing craft or academic knowledge is no longer seen as a solid enough basis on which to teach their specialisms. The latter group may present particular challenges as far as mentoring is concerned.

Post-compulsory institutions

As far as the institutional setting for the activity of mentoring is concerned, when referring to 'colleges' in this guide I am addressing mentors who are working with trainees in settings as diverse as:

- sixth-form colleges;
- general further education colleges;
- 'land-based' colleges specialising in agriculture and/or horticulture;
- adult colleges and adult education institutes;
- community and outreach settings, e.g. hostels for the homeless;
- private training institutions, especially those delivering contracted or franchised courses which are equally likely to be on offer in any of the above institutions.

To reiterate, there exists a 'package' of trainable, generic mentoring skills that may be deployed in any of these post-compulsory environments. A mentor gaining experience, and refining his/her skills, in a general FE college would be unlikely to be daunted by the prospect of working in any of the other types of institutions on the list.

Note

I have chosen to use throughout this guide the term 'trainee' in connection with the mentoring of any mentee (itself a possible alternative choice, of course), either on a full-time pre-service course or on one or other of the many variants of part-time programmes now being offered. (Far more trainees attend these each year than follow full-time programmes.) 'Student teacher' is still used by some institutions in connection with the first type of course, while others have adopted usages such as 'beginning teacher'. Both of these terms may, of course, be rejected by college staff following in-service courses, especially where they have already taught for any length of time.

In the literature of mentoring – much of which originates in the sphere of business and management, in particular US business – the use of 'protégé' is quite common. This has little currency in the context of PCET in the UK, so has been avoided in this guide. The idea of 'internship' may gain popularity, and at least one highly prestigious training provider has designated its (secondary PGCE) trainees as 'interns'. The most important reason for preferring 'trainee' is simply that of consistency with the language of OfSTED/ALI and DfES publications relating to training for the college sector.

The post-compulsory sector itself is increasingly being described in official documents as a Learning and Skills sector. However, I have not adopted this terminology in the guide as it appears that, to date, it is not actually being adopted by a wider constituency, including the majority of college teachers. In many ways, the simple notion that 'further education is everything that does not happen in schools or universities' (Kennedy 1997: 1) has much to commend it, and some readers may therefore feel that the use of 'FE' should have been opted for here.

References

DfES (2004) *Equipping Our Teachers for the Future: Reforming Initial Teacher Training for the Learning and Skills Sector.* Nottingham: Department for Education and Skills.

DfES (2005) 14–19 Education and Skills White Paper. Nottingham: Department for Education and Skills.

Freidson, E. (2001) *Professionalism: The Third Logic.* Cambridge: Polity Press.

Kennedy, Baroness H. (1997) *Learning Works. Widening Participation in Further Education.* Coventry: Further Education Funding Council.

Kingston, P. (2004) 'Equal but different'. *The Guardian*, 21 November
[Accessed at http://www.educationguardian.co.uk].

Mentoring in context

Chapter objectives:

- To examine the background to mentoring in colleges.
- To seek parallels with mentoring in other settings.
- To propose an appropriate 'architecture' for the activity.

> Mr Tollmun-Jones would despise anything I am associated with, because he can't stand me. I can't blame him; I'd loathe me if I had to try teaching me algebra – but I would start by telling me what the point of it is. He never has and I'm not very enthusiastic about pointless subjects.
>
> (Christopher Metcalfe, public schoolboy, in Corlett 1995)

It is probably essential, first, to elaborate on some of the background to this book, to outline the reasons why there is a place for a guide to mentoring in colleges, and what, as with algebra, the *point* of it is. We can probably group such reasons under three broad headings:

1. Political and organisational shifts relating to post-compulsory education and training (PCET).
2. Trends within professions and society generally.
3. Models of professional learning and development relating specifically to mentoring teachers in PCET.

The third of these areas is of such importance that it will be the *principal focus* of Chapter 3. Before dealing briefly with the first two of these points, to try to establish some relevance to mentors' actual roles, and therefore to find the 'point' of the guide, let us first note that mentoring, at least as far as the college sector is concerned, has until very recently been a significantly sidelined area. In an important text published in 1999, on FE in the twenty-first century

(Green and Lucas 1999), there are no index entries for 'mentor' or 'mentoring', nor is there much attention paid to the activity in the first FENTO – approved book on teaching in the sector (Wallace 2001). In the latter volume, mentors' contributions to initial teacher training would appear to consist merely of the provision of a lesson evaluation or a 'witness statement' for a trainee. The topic fares somewhat better in one of the best practical texts on college teaching (Huddleston and Unwin 2002 [2nd edn]), although even here we are only looking at five or so sentences.

However, there can be little doubt that the marginal attention paid thus far to mentoring within teacher training will *not* continue to be the case. With an estimated 20,000 teachers a year now needing to be trained for the newly designated learning and skills sector (DfES 2004) and the 'ideal state' being that each and every one of these individuals will be supported by a mentor, the sheer scale of the activity will be huge in comparison to what was observable only a decade or so ago.

Therefore I would claim that it is now worth adding to what is a small body of work on mentoring in the sector and to begin by reviewing selected developments in the first two of the three areas listed above. It is not hard to justify doing so: mentors' work is not undertaken in a vacuum, but has a *context*, a set of *origins*, and is probably most effective where its *conceptual basis* is acknowledged (the last of these, as mentioned previously, is examined in Chapter 3).

Political and organisational shifts relating to PCET

Teaching in colleges has probably never before presented the range of challenges that it does currently. Writing in 1998, Jocelyn Robson observed that:

> The nature of teaching in FE has always varied enormously and continues to vary within the different curriculum areas. As the sector has expanded its provision, so its character has become more complex and the demands upon teachers have increased.
> (Robson 1998: 591)

Half a dozen or so years on (and with now an annual total of approximately six million students studying in the post-compulsory sector) the complexity and demands are even greater. This is not the most appropriate place in which to offer a review and analysis of the dramatic changes we are witnessing (and those still in store), but suffice it to say that there are very few, if any, of these that are not directly impacting on new entrants to the teaching profession.

Acknowledging a growing recognition of the importance of initial teacher training in ensuring consistency in the quality of college provision for learners, the government, by its statutory instrument of 2001, introduced the requirement that training courses be followed by all new entrants.

This was one of many policy shifts aimed at rectifying the 'benign neglect' which Young *et al.* (1995) considered the college sector to have suffered from historically. It is possible to trace the subsequent growth of a real awareness of how college teachers play a pivotal role in the UK education system. Key documents such as the DfEE's *Colleges for Excellence and Innovation* stated forcefully why it was that far greater attention needed to be paid to:

> the development of the teaching staff, and senior management, in further education. It is they who are the essential resource who make the difference between learning which fails in achieving its objectives and that which is effective . . . we [cannot] continue in a situation where too many further education teachers have no formal qualifications or where, in too many cases, professional development is still insufficiently embedded in a culture of continuous improvement.
>
> (DfEE 2000: 24–5)

The major survey report compiled in 2003 by OfSTED is essential reading for anyone wishing to identify a key point in the transition from the 'before' of teacher training for PCET and its present state (and near-certain future). The report set out to review the quality of FE teacher training and made a number of quite critical observations: the summary of the report's findings actually begins by stating that:

> the current system of FE teacher training does not provide a satisfactory foundation of professional development for FE teachers at the start of their careers. While the tuition that trainees receive on the taught elements of their courses is generally good, few opportunities are provided for trainees to learn how to teach their specialist subjects, and there is *a lack of systematic mentoring* and support in the workplace. (OfSTED 2003: 5, emphasis added)

The importance attached to enhancing subject-specific mentoring is evident, and the recommendations made in this regard – and in many others which cannot be dealt with here – were unequivocally endorsed by the Standards Unit of the DfES in the following year (DfES 2004). As can easily be imagined, the reverberations of the OfSTED survey have been of very great significance in teacher training circles, but so too will they be for PCET institutions hosting or employing trainees. Mentoring will occupy a far more central position from now on.

Issues of quality and student entitlement

Issues of quality in teacher training, and of teacher quality itself, are intrinsically related to broader concerns within the sector – especially 'the quality of the learner experience' it provides. Colleges, ever since becoming independent corporations in 1993 (following the Further and Higher Education Act 1992), have devoted a considerable proportion of their energies to raising quality and achievement levels, with virtually all conceding that doing so hinges, first and foremost, on their human resources – teachers in particular, who are 'at the chalkface', or those (especially since 1997) 'involved in delivering' to learners.

Richard Gorringe, in a much-quoted phrase, referred to post-incorporation colleges being in the business of 'attracting, retaining and delighting paying customers' (1994, in Spours and Lucas 1996; Cunningham 1997: 6), the customers, of course, being students. In the highly competitive, target-driven environment in which colleges have had to operate since 1993, the aim of providing such services which, if not actually 'delighting' the student body, at least meet their *entitlements*, has been absolutely crucial in understanding the ethos of post-compulsory education.

Such important innovations as, first, a Charter for Further Education (DFE 1993) and then the adoption by each individual college of its own Student Charter laid out for prospective and current students what they could expect from their studies and from the staff who would support them in those studies. Such documents provide, in effect, 'checklists' against which the actual experience of college life can be measured. Where there is a misalignment, i.e. where what is being delivered fails to match what has been promised, students are actively encouraged to draw this to the attention of relevant staff and/or bodies. Mentors can, incidentally, very usefully provide trainees with a copy of their own college charter (alongside the other kinds of materials detailed in the relevant section of this guide). This can, fairly obviously, give a trainee insights into how their learners might be viewing, and evaluating, their performance.

There has been, as with most 'quality related' initiatives which have impacted on PCET, some debate about whether the dawning of the charter era has actually effected any real improvements in the student experience, or merely signalled the arrival of another set of high-minded, 'ought to have' statements. Yet in a number of quite specific ways it is hard to argue with what most charters tend to say about, for instance, the nature of the grading and comments students can expect to receive following the submission of assignments. Who would quibble with an undertaking to learners that 'work is assessed regularly and promptly. You will be kept informed of your progress' (Coleg Glan Hafren, n.d.). The high degree of importance attached to speedy, formative feedback on written work – say within a three-week period – absolutely accords with sound educational thinking on such issues. Similarly, an emphasis on supporting students' *individual* learning needs is very much in line with what research tells us enhances the quality of learning.

Students, it is true, may not always actually read such college materials as charters, but entitlement-related material often also appears in their handbooks (whether college- or course-specific ones) which usually *are* read. Most college prospectuses make explicit claims regarding what level of support tutors will provide. We may perhaps feel that these sorts of documents may breed a 'culture of complaint', but viewed more positively, they not only empower students but also serve to underscore what in the wider educational community is seen only as good practice.

The relevance of all this to mentors is that their trainees may well need to have, and will probably benefit from having, an element of their induction focused on student entitlement within the specific placement or employing institution. It may well be that this fulfils the useful purpose of pre-empting any possible observations by trainees regarding the 'demanding' students they might encounter.

With the advent of a much larger presence within colleges of the 14–16 age group, as new opportunities open up for school pupils in this age band to access the PCET curriculum, there will be many more issues arising, it seems likely, to do with college teachers being *in loco parentis*. In such a context mentors will be yet further challenged to adequately support new entrants who may find that colleges are far more diverse environments than they might have presupposed.

Trends within professions and society generally

The school sector

The fairly obvious place to start when reviewing developments in other professional areas is to look at the school sector and to make some comparisons with our own. Doing so has, arguably, a special value in the current climate of curricular change and the emergence of '14–19' as a key component of what comprises the UK education system. If there are approaches to mentoring being adopted in the school sector – which has a far better established tradition in this area – then we may well stand to profit from the sector's experience.

One very real difference between schools and colleges is that very few teachers in the former will be undergoing their training in-service, whereas this is the training mode which accounts for, by far, the greatest proportion of our own trainees. A second area of difference lies in the existence of formal 'probationary year' arrangements for new school teachers. (In the future, incidentally, this may be a development seen in colleges; the DfES certainly has the authority to introduce it, under the Education Act 2002, but for the present is 'holding [this] in reserve' (DfES 2004: 14).)

Such differences lead, for example, to a situation in which school-based mentors are far more actively involved in the assessment of trainees' written and other tasks which they must complete before qualifying. The differences also mean that, at least for their first year of teaching (the 'NQT year', i.e. the newly qualified teacher year), new entrants have an actual entitlement to support and mentoring. These kinds of things mean that the 'jurisdiction' of mentors, as well as their status, is enhanced. In addition, it seems true that school-based mentoring is presently more likely to be incentivised both financially and in terms of career advancement.

Other professional settings

Alongside what we can witness in the schools sector, however, it is worth mentioning the kinds of trends evident in other spheres of professional life. In business and commerce, for example, in an organisation such as the Royal Aeronautical Society (RAeS), mentoring principles and practices appear to be very fully embedded. The RAeS has adopted guidelines produced by the Engineering Council to produce its own guidance notes, to which adherence by members is expected. These guidelines stress such facets of mentoring practice as 'developing a close relationship with [trainees] . . . assessing them regularly, and . . . providing tuition and guidance as necessary' (RAeS 2001).

Mentors working to RAeS guidelines will work with three or four trainees at any one time, and are very strongly encouraged to 'remember there are other mentors' from whom learning can be derived and to 'use the relationship for [their] own development too' (ibid.). So positive is this particular organisation's conception of the benefits of mentoring that the guidelines end with the note that:

> We encourage mentoring for at least two years of the trainee's career, but there is no reason why it should stop, and indeed *it is preferable that it should continue beyond that time.* If you both find the relationship worthwhile and rewarding then we would encourage you to continue to meet.   (ibid., emphasis added)

There seems to be much food for thought for the PCET sector in such a strong endorsement of mentoring, especially over a longer time period than is common in education; and it is not only in the organisation named here that mentoring has been given a high profile; the same situation is discernible in a growing range of other non-educational settings, but a guide of this length cannot attempt to adequately describe this trend.

Mentoring in the community

We should also at least acknowledge the ways in which mentoring has been adopted by certain segments of the wider community to assist in the raising of standards and aspirations. The initiatives within Black and Minority Ethnic (BME) communities are especially interesting. A number of these fall within the broad ideal of 'mentoring for social inclusion', or what has been described as 'engagement mentoring' (Colley 2003: 2). This type of activity has focused on – as the term implies – preventing young people's *dis*engagement with school and/or society, or *re*-engaging those who have already, in one way or another, 'dropped out' as a result of their disaffection or inability to progress. As a variant of mentoring it has relied largely on volunteers and has been strongly associated with the kinds of outreach in the 'non-participant' community promoted by New Labour since 1997.

It is such a community which is being, at the time of writing, depicted in a poster campaign devised by a north London local authority endeavouring to reduce the incidence of car crime: 'male mentors' are sought to work with young men at risk of beginning the anti-social – and highly dangerous – activity of 'joy riding'.

Each of the above small number of illustrations simply serves to show how the diversity of contexts in which mentoring is now being encountered is large and growing. Even within colleges themselves, alongside the type of mentoring on which this guide will concentrate, we may find in existence:

- student 'buddy' systems (i.e. peer mentoring);
- the mentoring of current students by previous, successful, ones;
- mentoring by representatives of academic institutions (usually universities) aimed at promoting applications from under-represented groups; and
- employers assisting potential new recruits' readiness to successfully confront their selection procedures.

Mentors to teacher trainees are, to sum up, not alone in devoting a portion of their energies to supporting the learning and development of others. Mentoring is an area of rapidly growing importance and interest, and in certain respects appears – certainly in the context of teacher training and development – to be an excellent case of 'an idea whose time has come'. 'Mentoring is more than a fad' according to one source (Johnson and Ridley 2004: xv) and another goes even further in contending that 'Everyone needs a Mentor' (Clutterbuck 2001).

An 'architecture' for mentoring

Whether or not we would accept the validity of the observations with which the foregoing section is concluded, in particular that '*everyone* needs a mentor', I would argue strongly that *effective mentoring needs solid institutional backing.* Many analogies or metaphors would be possible here – from the 'fertile seedbeds' out of which mentoring might 'grow and develop', through the right 'climate' in which mentoring will 'thrive', to 'powerful motors' which will 'propel mentoring forward'. Having encountered and considered a number of such notions, I feel that none offers quite as much scope for describing and addressing mentors' needs within the organisations in which they practise as that of an 'institutional architecture'. This can encompass issues ranging from quotidian practicalities to far-reaching strategic matters.

As well as attempting to point to some useful definitional components of mentoring, and alluding to its potential for endowing professional benefits on both parties involved, we should, therefore, consider the institutional conditions – or *architecture* – likely to be conducive to the activity. This is a worthwhile exercise for a number of reasons, but for one in particular: as well as planning to identify and enhance individual capacities for mentoring it is essential to consider how institutional capacity will be supportive of the activity. Furthermore, it also seems fairly self-evident that if mentors are thinking about the 'ought' of mentoring (as in what ought to be in place to support them) they will be better equipped to campaign, should they so choose, over any marked institutional deficiencies.

For mentoring to be effective within an organisation, the individuals involved need to be adequately supported by what we might conceive of as the *architecture* of the activity. Put simply, the term as used here describes those 'design features' that support rather than constrain the work of mentors. In the same way that so-called 'sick' (i.e. badly designed) buildings are sometimes held to be responsible for lack of productivity, poor staff morale, high levels of absenteeism etc., so, too, might an organisation lacking the appropriate architecture be prone to ineffective, undervalued mentoring.

A number of key factors can be considered to be involved in ensuring that mentoring takes place within a well-designed environment – an organisation where 'the architecture is right'. Although the post-compulsory sector is an extremely variegated one, containing a great diversity of places of learning and training, it is still possible to identify factors of generic, overarching significance, and it is these that are summarised below.

An institutional commitment to mentoring

Mentors must believe that their efforts are recognised and rewarded. This, at a very basic level, would probably entail their being given a small amount of release from their own weekly classroom (or other 'management') commitments. More positively, an involvement in mentoring might be a criterion for consideration in connection with promotions, or the award of Advanced Skills Practitioner status or similar organisation-specific designations.

Other fairly obvious ways in which institutions can express their commitment to the value of mentoring apply more to new appointees/staff following in-service ITE programmes. Such individuals could be offered a named mentor for either their first year of service or for the duration of their ITE course. (Such a notion is already extremely well established in the school sector.) It almost goes without saying that such trainees will need sympathetic timetabling and – ideally – a lower overall amount of teaching; again, this kind of general principle has long been established in the school sector.

One PCET institution which is actively seeking to embed mentoring is West Kent College (WKC); key goals of the activity are succinctly expressed as ensuring that 'new staff have a positive experience of their first weeks at the college, that we retain valuable staff and that students benefit' (WKC 2004).

An appropriate institutional ethos

The term 'collegiality' has probably become somewhat overworked, but the promotion of a collegial climate is certainly relevant to our notion of an appropriate architecture for mentoring. As a notion, collegiality has the real merit of encompassing the potential *reciprocity* of mentoring relationships. Mentors make their knowledge and skills available to less-experienced colleagues but, in turn, learn from them. Mentors' professional learning can be enhanced by the kinds of questions posed by trainees ('Yes, but why do you think that would be a useful strategy to use with this group?') and by the kinds of scenarios they are likely to present for discussion ('So what would you have done in that kind of situation?'). Mentors' understanding of their own professional practices and the legitimacy of these can only be deepened by the kinds of interaction alluded to here. Institutions would do well to take opportunities – e.g. in recruitment literature and staff handbooks – to make explicit the ways in which they are seeking to foster collegiality through mentoring.

A second valuable construct that can be drawn on (even if only rather superficially) in the value being attached to mentoring is that of 'communities of practice' (Lave and Wenger 1991). In the classic formulation of what is involved in such an entity, and using the perhaps rather daunting terminology 'legitimate peripheral participation', they describe how

> learners inevitably participate in communities of practitioners and . . . the mastery of knowledge and skill requires newcomers to move toward full participation in the socio-cultural practices of a community. 'Legitimate peripheral participation' provides a way to speak about the relations between newcomers and old-timers . . . It concerns the process by which newcomers become part of a community of practice. (ibid.: 29)

In our present context we can conceive of 'learners' as being the trainees, without in any way distorting the authors' original perspective. An institution which therefore actively promotes a community of practice and focused interaction between 'newcomers' and 'old-timers' is one that is highly likely to achieve 'full participation' by the former group. One of the ways in which Lave and Wenger add to our understanding of how learning takes place – for our purposes *professional* learning – is that they give special emphasis to the social, and in doing so open up a broad range of opportunities for institutions to develop communities of practice, rather than limit their strategies exclusively to those bounded by classroom walls.

Using somewhat similar terminology to 'communities of practice', the Department for Education and Skills has recently described the advantages of 'creating "professional learning communities" in colleges and providers' (DfES 2004). Here, too, we have an endorsement of the importance of its *ethos* in the *effectiveness* of a college or other PCET institution.

An institution such as West Kent College, mentioned above, has so strongly taken on board the importance of mentoring within its overall set of procedures that it has produced a commendably practical *Mentoring Policy*, and, moreover, has spelled out in this the way in which the mentoring scheme which has been devised should be considered in conjunction with:

- Quality Assurance policy.
- Induction procedure.
- Recruitment policy.
- Staff Development policy and procedures.
- Staff Review policy and procedures.
- Equal Opportunities policy.

(WKC 2004)

The advantages of thereby integrating mentoring within a wider set of 'architectural features' of the organisation are potentially very great; certainly there is minimal risk, it would seem, of mentoring being perceived by staff as in any way peripheral to the college's mission.

The physical resources for mentoring

Basic minimum requirements here would include the availability of a (preferably dedicated) meeting room in which such confidential activities as post-observation debriefings can take place. Mentors might also use this room as a venue for periodic discussions or occasional 'case conferences'. It might also be the most appropriate location for the kind of action learning sets whose functions I describe elsewhere in this guide.

In some institutional settings, electronic networking by mentors might be more realistic than face-to-face meetings, so facilitating this (e.g. by recommending use of college intranets where these have been created) should be prioritised. Institutions' financial resources might allow for the purchase of a small collection of relevant texts which mentors could borrow, and/or subscriptions to worthwhile professional journals.

Induction, training and support for mentors

The skills set needed by effective mentors should not be considered to be exactly the same as that displayed by *all* good teachers; there are certainly important overlaps, but no institution should take for granted the readiness to begin mentoring of even highly successful classroom practitioners. Induction of new mentors is essential (and, of course, is one further way in which institutional commitment to the endeavour can be communicated to staff).

The first dimension of induction should, ideally, comprise a clear articulation of the rationale for mentoring – how it accords with an institution's mission, its strategic plan, and how it should be viewed as fundamentally connected to 'the learner experience'. The centrality of the learner within the current inspection framework (OfSTED/ALI 2001) makes it essential that the role of mentoring in, ultimately, enhancing achievement is highlighted in the induction of mentors.

Also deserving of a prominent place within the rationale being presented for mentoring is an indication of how the activity will possibly be viewed by other 'stakeholders'. Here we are considering the value of having a sound mentoring scheme in place should there be external scrutiny in connection with such awards as Investors in People, or the various quality kitemarks which are seen in the sector as being worthwhile indicators of a healthy, successful organisation.

The kind of training provided at the induction stage should be underpinned by sound theoretical perspectives relevant to the activity of mentoring, but should also benefit from the inclusion of case studies, where these can be derived from teachers' professional biographies, which clearly indicate the credit which mentoring can be given for any improvements in professional practice.

It would be possible to write in great detail on the structure and content of mentor induction/training, but here I would only wish to highlight one additional highly desirable feature of such events. This is the prominence that would need to be given to classroom observation, given the increasing significance of this aspect of their roles which mentors will discern.

Induction should only, however, be seen as the first stage in the support of mentors and it will need to be supplemented by proper ongoing support. Such support can take the form of providing opportunities to share not only issues and concerns, but also successes and best practice.

In the contexts of both induction/training and ongoing support, there may well be an argument in favour of engaging external trainers/facilitators, rather than having senior staff take responsibility for organising and delivering events. It is possibly less likely for negative sentiments to be generated if outside contributors are used (management 'sermonising', then trying to use mentors in a surveillance operation to 'weed out' weak teachers); but clearly this is a highly debatable supposition.

The selection and accreditation of mentors

But who are the staff who will be inducted and trained as mentors? A useful perspective from the context of the school sector is that 'mentoring only flourishes when it is perceived by senior managers as an important aspect of staff development rather than a tiresome burden to be landed on unwilling and unprepared shoulders' (Stephens 1996: 4). We can, I hope, see the equal validity of this proposition when translated to colleges. First, mentors should ideally be selected, rather than 'landed with' the role, and here we arrive at one of the greatest challenges to institutions seeking to have their 'architecture' properly thought out. The post-compulsory sector appears (particularly since 1992) to have suffered disproportionately from poor morale, a perception by long-serving staff that the pressures of teaching have been greatly increased by the growth of an intrusive 'audit culture', by the advent of student entitlements and by the ever-increasing diversity of the cohort.

Furthermore, we are aware of a degree of 'innovation fatigue' being experienced by staff as one proposal for curriculum or accreditation reform seems to follow another. If, for the sake of argument, we accept this depiction of a teacher's life in the sector (which is not a wholly idiosyncratic one, as a reading of 'Why do they do it?' by McKelvey and Andrews (1998) could confirm), what might entice often beleaguered staff to commit themselves to becoming mentors? Rather than institutions being in the position of being able to *select* appropriate candidates for mentoring, might not the reality be that staff must in the main be *pressurised* into taking on the role? In some cases this could well be exactly what happens – or at any rate, subtle inducements are perhaps being provided so that institutional needs for an adequate pool of mentors can be met.

The heart of the challenge is in portraying mentoring as a desirable, worth-while activity with both personal and professional rewards attached to it. A starting point for constructing such a positive, attractive profile for the role ought really to start with the drawing up of appropriate selection criteria, and making it plain that status and kudos will accrue to individuals able to meet these. Institutions also need to actively seek arrangements with training providers and/or awarding bodies which would allow for the accreditation of mentoring as a high-level, work-based professional activity. Already universities with important interests in the post-compulsory sector allow for the accreditation (typically at Masters level) of such professional learning as derives from mentoring, with registration fees more often than not being paid by employing organisations in the sector.

By signalling such possibilities as these, the professional benefits of mentoring for mentors themselves, as well as trainees, are heavily underlined. As with certain other aspects of institutions demonstrating their commitment to mentoring, as outlined above, these kinds of initiatives seem to depend as much on will, and priorities, as on financial resources.

Issues of clarity and consistency

These two considerations are most sensibly reviewed together, as they are strongly interconnected. First, it seems self-evident that in the same way as selection criteria for intending mentors are necessary, so too is a clear specification of what exactly the role entails; in other words, mentoring needs a job description. What are the principal functions mentors are expected to fulfil, with what kind of frequency, and what kinds of documentation (if any) will they have to deal with?

Similarly, if mentors' obligations – and their entitlements – are being spelled out, so too should be those of trainees. The nature of mentors' and trainees' responsibilities, and the divisions between these, can even be embodied in a mentoring *contract* – which in its most formal guise would be signed by both parties. This kind of device allows for easy reference to the key dimensions of the mentoring relationship as being proposed within an organisation, and it can fulfil the very important function of elucidating the boundaries within which both parties are agreeing to act.

Whatever format is adopted for outlining 'who does what' (or ought to), it should ideally embody a set of ideas based on a *shared ownership* of these. A sometimes lengthy but ultimately worthwhile process is to establish a small working group of individuals from various levels of an institution to draft guidelines on which mentoring relationships should be founded – for evaluation after a specified period in use. This, to a reasonable degree, can militate against criticism of what is being proposed, and, in particular, will pre-empt the claim that any new procedures have merely been 'imposed by the management'.

While we must acknowledge that an overly rigid approach to the structure of mentoring could in itself be a factor promoting antagonism to any scheme, clearly a high-priority aim must be to ensure a good measure of consistency across departmental/curricular areas. A model of an overarching framework, or contract, setting out responsibilities and entitlements for both mentor and trainee, would be one in which there was some scope for 'good sense' flexibility and adjustments. But it would also have in-built guarantees of *minimum* levels of contact, support, observation and so on, no matter what the trainee's specialism. This can help ensure that any sense of grievance that emerges, where, say, a trainee feels they have not been provided with the same level of face-to-face time as a colleague has had with their mentor, can be discussed with reference to, and framed by, what has been approved as institutional policy by a number of stake-holders. Guidelines for good mentoring practice, to be readily discerned by their readers as promoting consistency across subject areas, must be written in an accessible way, must avoid ambiguity (while retaining the flexibility I am advo-cating) and should be regularly updated in the light of experience and evaluation.

The 'subject specificity' debate

The architecture of an institution's mentoring arrangements needs to be created in a way that is responsive to the increasingly strong criticism (OfSTED 2003) that trainees are not well served by mentoring which is wholly *generic*, and fails to recognise their needs for clear and expert guidance on the best ways in which to approach the particular challenges of teaching their own subject. According to the important survey carried out by OfSTED:

> The content of the [training] courses rarely includes the development of subject-specific pedagogy to equip new teachers with the specific knowledge and skills nec-essary for teaching their specialist subject or vocational area.   (OfSTED 2003: 6)

The traditionally generic nature of most training for post-compulsory teaching derives from the real difficulties in 'customising' the delivery of training to meet the individual needs of an enormously diverse range of specialists. There is a stark contrast between training for the secondary school sector, where providers generally need only accommodate new entrants to the profession preparing to teach one of the National Curriculum subjects. These individuals can be taught in groups of Modern Foreign Languages (MFL), Science, History or Maths specialists, for example – and almost always by tutors who have taught these same subjects in schools. It would be quite unnecessary to labour the point, but one of the truly distinctive attributes of the post-compulsory sector is the sheer number of subjects, courses and pathways that attract both learners and intending teachers. To date, it has only been viewed as feasible or desirable to create subject-specific training pathways (on something like the school teacher training model) in a very restricted range of areas – i.e. English for Speakers of Other Languages (ESOL) and Adult Basic Skills (ABS). The very special reasons which lie behind recent developments in these areas are to do with current government priorities (its strong desire to promote social inclusion and cohesion), a rapid growth in learner numbers creating almost unprecedented demand for appropriately trained ESOL and ABS specialists, and particular concerns having been expressed over a period of time regarding teaching quality and learners' achievements in ESOL and ABS.

In principle, the aspiration of trainees to be mentored by someone whose area of expertise closely matches their own is not hard to accept. Wherever feasible, mentoring by a co-specialist (or at least by someone from a disciplinary background cognate with that of the trainee) should be engineered. This, besides being compliant with what the Inspectorate would wish to see in place, is from most perspectives only sensible.

However, it is probably unrealistic to establish hard-and-fast rules on the matter in a number of institutions. Some may have tiny specialist departments, where the 'newcomer' (see above) is perhaps the only full-time member of staff. Elsewhere, no appropriately experienced staff within a department or section may be available. (A case comes to mind where some years ago I requested of a particular college department mentoring for a trainee on a full-time pre-service course only to be told that because of very high turnover, every single member of the team in that department would be new in post for the start of the academic year!)

In these kinds of problematic situations there appears little to recommend beyond attempting to negotiate mentoring by someone from another discipline, to be supplemented where possible by arranging access to subject-specific support outside the institution, e.g. in one of the subject groups/centres publicising their activities in special interest journals.

However, it is also well worth reminding ourselves at this point of two things. First, that all trainees will benefit from 'being introduced to wider professional issues' (Lucas 2004) and second, of the risks attached to professional learning 'being ghettoised into narrow, subject-based notions of teaching' (ibid.). In the very restricted domains of some vocational areas it is quite possible that 'narrow ways of teaching have become entrenched' (ibid.). For this reason we would probably be mistaken to seek a panacea for all the present perceived deficiencies in institutions' mentoring arrangements in the shape of subject-specificity.

Measuring the impact of mentoring

For any claims to be made at all about the effectiveness of a mentoring framework which has been put in place there needs to be some mechanism for researching this – for gathering data and making sense of it. This, then, is the last, but by no means least, important dimension of an 'architecture' for mentoring to which thought needs to be given.

If post-compulsory institutions are to become 'learning organisations' (which some already are), then they need to investigate every aspect of their practices. The current emphasis on self-evaluation, as required by the inspection framework for the sector, is of course of strong relevance here. Within the specific context of mentoring, however, the demands for data and analysis appear to be minimal. Therefore, a fuller picture should probably be sought, probably by such key personnel as those with major staff development responsibilities. Pursuing such a course can only lead to a better understanding of the components of effective mentoring practice. Logically, it will be most productive as a course of action if data are gathered from mentors, trainees,[1] and their supervisors/managers. Further, it has special potential to inform the kind of mentoring to be conducted in cases of teacher underperformance (such as those that surface because of student complaints) where the price to be paid for ineffective, poorly targeted mentoring can be high. Evaluation and monitoring of mentoring should produce the kind of concrete 'continuous quality improvement' which is being promoted across the sector, but especially in cases where teaching standards and learner achievement are causing concern (Kingston 2004).

Note

1. The use of focus groups of mentored trainees has been of special value to me as an external examiner to one university's PCET ITE programmes. The richness of the material that is often produced, given an appropriate degree of assurance regarding participants' confidentiality, is in my view hard to surpass. In focus groups, individuals can 'spark off each other', and we can see operating processes such as one member of the group further developing a point made by a peer. If there is a 'downside' to the use of this forum it might be the distorting effect caused by an over-dominant individual taking too much 'airtime' – focus groups can need as careful management as a learner group where such individuals are present.

References

Clutterbuck, D. (2001) *Everyone Needs a Mentor: Fostering Talent at Work* (3rd edn). London: Chartered Institute of Personnel and Development.

Coleg Glan Hafren (n.d.) Student Charter (3rd edn). Cardiff: Coleg Glan Hafren.

Colley, H. (2003) *Mentoring for Social Inclusion: A Critical Approach to Nurturing Mentoring Relationships.* London: RoutledgeFalmer.

Corlett, W. (1995) *Now and Then.* London: Abacus.

Cunningham, B. (1997) 'The failing teacher in further education'. *Journal of Further and Higher Education,* 21(3), 365–71.

DFE (1993) The Charter for Further Education. Nottingham: Department for Education.

DfEE (2000) *Colleges for Excellence and Innovation.* Nottingham: Department for Education and Employment.

DfES (2004) *Equipping Our Teachers for the Future: Reforming Initial Teacher Training for the Learning and Skills Sector*. Nottingham: Department for Education and Skills.

Gorringe, R. (1994) 'Changing the culture of a college'. *Coombe Lodge Report* cited in Spours, K. and Lucas, N. (1996) *The Formation of a National Sector of Incorporated Colleges: Beyond the FEFC Model*. London: Post-16 Education Centre, Institute of Education, University of London.

Green, A. and Lucas, N. (1999) *FE and Lifelong Learning: Realigning the Sector for the Twenty-first Century*. London: Bedford Way Papers, Institute of Education, University of London.

Huddleston, P. and Unwin, L. (2002) *Teaching and Learning in Further Education*. London: RoutledgeFalmer.

Johnson, W. B. and Ridley, C. R. (2004) *The Elements of Mentoring*. New York: Palgrave Macmillan.

Kingston, P. (2004) 'More colleges fail in south'. *Education Guardian*, 30 November.

Lave, J. and Wenger, E. (1991) *Situated Learning: Legitimate Peripheral Participation*. Cambridge: Cambridge University Press.

Lucas, N. (2004) 'When there are too few mentors in the pot'. *Times Educational Supplement*, FE focus, 21 May.

McKelvey, C. and Andrews, J. (1998) 'Why do they do it? A study into the perceptions and motivations of trainee further education lecturers'. *Research in Post-Compulsory Education*, 3(3), 357–67.

OfSTED/ALI (2001) *The Common Inspection Framework*. London: Office for Standards in Education/Adult Learning Inspectorate.

OfSTED (2003) *The Initial Training of Further Education Teachers: A Survey*. London: Office for Standards in Education [HMI 1762].

Robson, J. (1998) 'A profession in crisis: status, culture and identity in the further education college'. *Journal of Vocational Education and Training*, 50(4), 585–607.

RAeS (2001) *Guidance for Mentors*, May 2001. London: Royal Aeronautical Society.

Stephens, S. (1996) *Essential Mentoring Skills*. Cheltenham: Stanley Thornes.

Wallace, S. (2001) *Teaching and Supporting Learning in Further Education*. Exeter: Learning Matters.

WKC (2004) *Mentoring Policy*, May 2004. Tonbridge: West Kent College.

Young, M., Lucas, N., Sharp, G. and Cunningham, B. (1995) *Teacher Training for the FE Sector: Training the Lecturer of the Future*. London: Post-16 Education Centre, Institute of Education, University of London.

The effective mentor's skills, attributes and functions

Chapter objective:

- To specify the core activities of mentoring, and the most appropriate attributes and skills for undertaking these.

> Teachers change in countless ways during the process of their careers . . . They become more experienced, at least in the sense of having taught for a longer time. They often learn new skills. They do things better. They become more knowledgeable . . . They sometimes become more patient, wise and witty. Some of them, however, become discouraged, fatigued, 'burnt out', cynical, lazy. A few of them go dotty.
>
> (Philip W. Jackson)

The above quotation (from 'Helping teachers develop', in Hargreaves and Fullan's (1992) excellent *Understanding Teacher Development* – a source of real value to all observers of teaching) – nicely draws attention to the wisdom and patience that experienced teachers acquire over the years. These two attributes are as valuable as any that mentors are likely to possess. On the other hand, one would hope that most practising or intending mentors are not afflicted by any of the negatives that are mentioned – although who has not experienced a natural fatigue after a full day's teaching into which a great deal of energy has been put? Possessing positive *attributes*, or 'dispositions', is an enormously important foundation for the development of mentoring *skills*. What I shall focus on in this chapter, however, is not only these skills and attributes but also how they come into play in the actual job of mentoring – performing the functions attached to the role.

Mentoring: definitions and specifications

Most mentors would probably quite readily be able to note down a few points they would work into an explanation of what exactly it is they feel they have taken on. However, it would probably be surprising if at this early stage some kind of working definition of the activity were not provided, and I would therefore propose the following:

> **Mentors in PCET are skilled, experienced teachers who are involved in guiding, counselling and supporting trainees in practical ways. They are able to offer both a role model and essential information on a college's learners, its curriculum, its organisational structure and its policies, at least those relating to learning and teaching.**

Clearly, this is at one and the same time a definition more tightly focused than one to be found in a dictionary (e.g. usually something along the lines of 'wise teacher') and significantly different from one relating to the specifics of a different occupational area, many of which tend to stress 'coaching' as being at the heart of mentoring.

Many training institutions adopt more succinct versions of what is involved in mentoring trainees, the University of Cardiff, for example, simply stating that 'a mentor will be an experienced subject specialist and a classroom teacher' (Cardiff University 2003). The Further Education Training Organisation emphasises, in its own materials, that a mentor should be 'an excellent teacher . . . [who] can encourage others towards excellence' (FENTO 2001: 1), indicating ways in which mentors ought to *stand out* from other practitioners. And a standard text on teaching in the sector opts for the equally to-the-point, 'an experienced member of staff who provides ongoing support, advice and guidance' (Huddleston and Unwin 2002).

A number of colleges are themselves also involved in the delivery of initial teacher education and they have attempted to define what mentoring entails (as have some colleges that are not so involved but who are nevertheless putting staff mentoring schemes in place). West Kent College's mentoring policy, and their efforts in this regard, are described elsewhere in this guide.

So there is a range of possible ways of encapsulating what mentoring comprises, and it would probably be fruitless to try to find a superiority in any one perspective on the activity. Largely as a result of the very large number of professional spheres in which mentoring has been initiated (and subsequently researched by academics) it is exceptionally difficult to claim that any one definition has an all-encompassing, comprehensive validity. Some years ago, Healy and Welchert (1990) described a 'definitional conundrum' arising from a tension between classical notions of long-term (often spontaneous and based on goodwill) mentoring relationships and those which are 'on the other hand . . . assigned, short-term, cost-effective arrangements of limited significance' (p. 18). While it is clear that virtually all the 'arrangements' with which readers of this guide will be concerned will generally fall into this latter category, they can certainly possess *very real significance* for both parties.

Given the prominence that is being given in initial teacher education to *reflective practice* (see Chapter 3) it seems only logical to highlight, early on, the strong desirability of mentors themselves being in sympathy with the notion. Reflective practitioners are also those endowed with the wisdom and patience to which Jackson refers; they are the experienced teachers who still, after however many years, mentally review classes they have taught, are sensitive to things that did not go as well as they may have wanted, and are thinking ahead constructively to implement refinements. The mentor who is a reflective practitioner will be most able to empathise with trainees' anxieties, I would contend, because they remain far from complacent or blasé about their own performance in the classroom; in short, they have not stopped reflecting on, and learning about, teaching.

At the risk of standing accused of veering too far into the realm of popular psychology, it may also be the case that effective mentors are individuals whose 'emotional intelligence' (as a great number of writers are now referring to a particular set of perspectives) is well developed. They are not only self-aware regarding feelings – what antagonises or hurts, for instance – but are adept at gauging how their words and actions will be experienced by, in the present, trainees they are mentoring. They are, to put it simply, sensitive and considerate; they also find it possible, emotionally, to accommodate without distress a view of the world that may be at odds with their own. Alongside seeking to effect change and improvement in their trainees, they are themselves open to change in their own attitudes and behaviours, accepting that the professional learning arising from a mentoring relationship may not be an exclusively one-sided process.

Effective mentors are also probably the kinds of individuals who would fall within Hoyle's (1974) conception of *extended professionals*, i.e. teachers who embrace involvements with professional activities beyond those of teaching in their own classrooms (in contrast to the group Hoyle defined as *restricted* professionals, or those individuals falling within Carr's (1992) notion of 'procedural' professionals). They may, too, be inclined to assume *activist* (Sachs 2001) roles; for example, rigorously advocating for their trainees in various quarters, or campaigning for the creation, where it does not already exist, of the kind of 'architecture' described in Chapter 1.

All of the above notions may, perhaps, point to the existence of a 'mentoring mindset', but in certain respects, some of them are simply what we can recognise as the defining characteristics of any person-centred professional activity. Mentors – most especially new ones – will probably, and entirely understandably, focus more on the practicalities of what will be required of them than on contemplating these ideas, and useful sources of guidance here are, first, the materials provided by teacher training institutions, principally universities (and increasingly by colleges themselves) and, second, the perceptions and expectations of new trainees as they emerge as a result of academic research. There is little to be gained here by attempting to summarise in any meaningful way what trainers are currently stipulating: each mentor will need to adhere closely to the specific requirements of a particular training scheme. However, some recently expressed views of trainees themselves may provide a helpful depiction of the kinds of expectations with which mentors can be faced.

What the trainees say they need

Certain themes may be seen to emerge from a collation of anonymous responses gathered over a recent four-year period (to 2004) to questions posed to trainees regarding what they hope a mentor will provide for them, and what facets of mentoring they view as essential. The kinds of perceptions held are shown below; to avoid a large amount of repetition many responses from the trainee cohorts concerned are left uncited, but, as indicated, the most important themes can be illustrated on the basis of those statements that are used. There is no particular priority implied by the order in which the list has been compiled:

- 'genuine concern for my development';
- 'support and encouragement';
- 'I hope my mentor is, most importantly, a good teacher whom the students respect and who I can be inspired by and learn from';
- 'will give me continuous feedback whether good or bad';
- 'somebody who will keep me involved from the outset, and make clear what is expected of me';
- 'someone who takes a genuine interest in me as an individual, as well as a trainee';
- 'approachable and willing to give constructive criticism';
- 'consistent support, structure and guidance';
- 'will set me realistic and achievable aims';
- 'someone who will be friendly and put me at my ease in a new environment';
- 'an understanding of my abilities, strengths and weaknesses';
- 'comfortable about expressing opinions about what I can do to improve';
- 'subject-specific help about how to present particular topics'.

One thing which may well strike readers is the degree of openness conveyed by a number of these verbatim statements; there is plentiful evidence of willingness to learn, and a real acceptance of the fact that criticisms from mentors will form part of the transaction. Trainees are overwhelmingly receptive to being mentored. High value is being attached to the services of a mentor, a starting point that would be hard to improve on – but one that may occasionally be experienced by mentors as somewhat challenging.

To complement these kinds of statements regarding trainees' *needs*, it might be useful at this point to attempt to raise mentors' awareness of the kinds of *anxieties* they frequently bring with them. Again, I present here only a relatively small selection of the kinds of issues raised anonymously in similar exercises, over a similar period, to those which produced the statements in the list above. Nevertheless, they are highly representative of the kinds of recurrent themes we encounter.

Trainees' anxieties

- 'Being assessed, e.g. teaching the class and being observed on my performance then graded';
- '[Teaching] groups of mixed ability and motivation';
- 'I hope I will be sufficiently knowledgeable in my subject area to be able to teach it to the required standard';
- 'I hope I can stand up and teach in front of a room full of people';
- 'I am concerned about how much time we will have to prepare our first lessons once we know what subject matter it is we will have to teach';
- 'A little frightened about my own knowledge [and] questions that students might have – not being able to answer immediately';
- 'concerned about maintaining a high level of self-confidence';
- 'I think I'm going to look younger than most of my students';
- '[Getting] a good job at the end';
- 'Standing up and presenting material. Does it get easier?';
- 'Generating interest and a stimulating, animated classroom environment from dry, theoretical, subject matter'.

These, then, are the sorts of things, the needs and the anxieties, around which mentors will want to devise appropriate supportive strategies. In doing so, their own skills and attributes may sometimes allow them to take this in their stride; at other times (and in particular in the context of the problem-focused mentoring dealt with later in this guide) they may feel really quite stretched. Possessing the kinds of 'CV items' described below will undoubtedly be a solid foundation, one which can be built on over many years of mentoring practice.

A 'CV' for mentoring

Mentors working in the specific context of supporting trainee teachers will ideally be endowed with a range of skills such as those described below. As will become evident, the list strongly corresponds to one that could be collated on the basis of the kinds of sentiments and perceptions of trainees summarised above.

Proven effectiveness in the classroom

Skills in this area may not exclusively have been judged solely on the basis of exam results, although as a consideration these may well be taken into account. Other highly relevant measures of effectiveness can be said to include student satisfaction, as indicated by evaluations and surveys; retention rates; and – more subjectively – simply the kind of credit and esteem colleagues tend to confer when someone becomes known as an engaging and popular teacher. It might be that the classroom skill and expertise of a mentor has already been acknowledged formally within an institution, and they may, for example, hold 'beacon', 'champion' or 'advanced skills' status (all designations currently being encountered, among others).

Management skills

The term here is being used in a very broad sense, to encompass such areas of professional life as course design and management (often taken to include seeking accreditation for, or verification of, a programme, oversight of exam entry procedures, organising the purchase of relevant course materials etc.).

Mentors who are adept at file management, coping with the demands of a data-hungry environment, and who have an ability to remain unperturbed by deadlines – and to meet them – may also be advantaged because the mentoring function carries an increment of paperwork in the form of reports to be sub- mitted by advised dates and so on. All phases of education are now, in their own slightly different ways, *audit cultures*, and being able to peacefully coexist with this fact – if we cannot embrace it – is important.

The ability to form and maintain effective professional relationships

This dimension of mentoring lies at its very heart. To support and enhance the professional development of a trainee entails, at its most basic level, being able to get on with them and encouraging them to feel positive about working with a mentor. 'As with many of the roles that support experiential learning, it succeeds or fails on the basis of the relationship that is established between the mentor and mentee' (Fry *et al.* 1999: 145).

There is, of course, a risk attached to stressing, in a guide such as this, 'relationships'; the term can connote an emotional intensity, loyalty and commitment which are very rarely, if ever, going to be as appropriate in mentoring as they would be in certain other contexts. Nevertheless, the justification for referring to the notion is easily located in the frequency with which *unsuccessful* mentor–trainee 'pairings' are described by trainees in the language of 'failed', 'bad', 'negative' or 'unhealthy' relationships.

Some, at least, of the positive characteristics of good personal relationships probably do have a transferability to mentor–trainee ones – respect, reliability, honesty, tolerance of failings and a measure of flexibility all come to mind.

High-level communication skills

'He knows his subject, but really gets in a mess trying to say what he wants to say.'

In certain essentials, mentoring draws on key *teaching* skills: the mentor is coaching, advising and guiding 'their' trainee. These activities, to have successful outcomes, all call for such staples of the teacher's repertoire as being able to pitch information at an appropriate level, avoiding pretentious or jargon-ridden expositions and actively inviting requests for restatement or clarification where necessary. All good teachers also place emphasis on what is most significant, are self-aware of any potentially offensive phrasing (whether culturally, socially or sexually) and are alert to the risks posed by ambiguity.

As the educationist Lewis Elton often expresses it, when identifying what is at the heart of effective teaching, it is the ability of the expert to *translate* their knowledge in such a way as to make it accessible to the uninitiated. This simple concept not only ought to inform our teaching in the most fundamental of ways but it also seems to offer a great deal to an understanding of the nature of effective, positive mentoring.

An ability to counsel

In another educational context, that of personal tutoring, Waterhouse (1991) presents a strong case for this activity depending on a mix (shown in his text as a 'tennis court'-like diagram) of skills borrowed from both teaching and counselling. I would argue that a similar proposition has validity when applied to mentoring. From the traditional set of *teaching* skills mentors draw on their ability to describe and explain, to set out alternatives, to underline the significance of certain facts and principles, and so on. From *counselling*, they find themselves, for instance, using their listening skills, empathising with difficulties being experienced and supportively drawing out what trainees might actually be feeling (perhaps sometimes in contrast to what they *say* they are feeling). It is this kind of overlap which my own depiction in Figure 2.1 – rather more like a Venn diagram than Waterhouse's original – attempts to encapsulate.

It is not in any sense being implied here that mentors need to have pursued a course of psychotherapeutic counselling training before they can be considered qualified to assume their responsibilities (and of course it needs to be noted that there are dangers in attempting to be 'real' counsellors to our trainees without having had the benefit of such training; there is, in particular, the issue of *professional boundaries* to be considered). I am simply indicating that certain basic, strongly humanistic elements of counselling practice can be of value to mentors in their work. As teachers, many probably do possess well-honed listening skills and are ever receptive and attuned to their learners' anxieties. It is highly likely that the majority of practising mentors have previously held responsibilities as personal tutors to learner groups, and many will continue to work in this setting while also mentoring. It is, therefore, simply the probability that mentors will connect with a 'tutoring-derived' model that leads to its inclusion here.

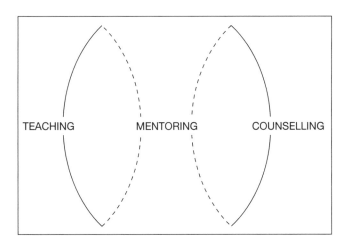

Figure 2.1 Teaching and counselling: overlapping skills for mentoring (adapted from Waterhouse 1991: 8)

Strong subject knowledge

Elsewhere in this guide the present overwhelmingly *generic* nature of much training for the post-compulsory sector is stressed. Against this backdrop, the very special and highly valued contributions of the subject specialist cannot be over-emphasised. The designation 'Curriculum Mentor' adopted on some training schemes in itself signals the distinctiveness of the role and its responsibilities. The term 'Subject Co-Tutor' is one that would give even greater prominence to the desired subject-specificity of mentoring, but as yet this has primarily been favoured within the context of training for the school sector.

Being an expert in one's subject allows for much more than, say, simply being able to tell a trainee that there has been an inaccuracy in some factual material they have been teaching – which is not to dismiss the importance of doing so where necessary. Subject expertise, combined with length of teaching the subject, means that mentors can provide inputs to which it is highly unlikely trainees will obtain access in other quarters. In particular, mentors ought, in principle, to be able to:

- recommend the most up-to-date and valuable sources of subject knowledge which trainees can draw on. Such sources can encompass texts, professional journals, electronic sources and courses/conferences;

- offer advice, on the basis of experience, concerning which elements of topics/texts/assignments have tended to cause learners most difficulty. This will enhance the ability of trainees to target their efforts, both in the classroom and when designing and producing learning materials, so that special emphasis is given to supporting learners with areas which have apparently presented barriers;

- provide insights into such practical considerations as how much time it has been demonstrated learners ought to spend on the various parts of a syllabus to ensure success;

- induct trainees into the specifics of relevant accreditation in their subject, so that trainees can confidently approach the business of preparing their learners for major assessment hurdles. For mature entrants, in particular, the differences between now and, say, the 1980s in terms of the organisation and 'badging' of examinations are often perplexing and they will tend to need a lot of support in understanding the present landscape of credentials and assessment strategies;

- allow access to their own classes, so that the observation of teaching becomes a two-way process. Trainees can learn a vast amount from the observation of a skilled, experienced teacher of their own specialism – seeing the pacing, pitch and style of a professional teacher at work is a priceless opportunity, and one which will probably come about only extremely rarely in the first years of a new entrant's career in PCET;

● simply share their enthusiasm for their subject, and demonstrate that it is not inevitable that after a given period staleness and cynicism will set in.

It is, finally, worth noting that an even greater emphasis is likely to be placed on subject-specificity in mentoring as the reforms comprising the government's Success for All agenda begin to be more consequential for mentors. What is sought is: '. . . in particular approaches to mentoring to help teachers develop teaching skills in their own specialist or subject area' (DfES 2004: 4).

While the contributions which can be made by generic mentoring (e.g. as offered by trainees' personal tutors) are acknowledged in recent policy documents, it is undoubtedly the role of subject-specific mentoring that is now in the ascendant. New, and somewhat more generous, funding arrangements, ostensibly to be in place by 2007 (ibid.), will formalise the greater responsibilities being placed on colleges to organise the recruitment, training and support of mentors from across the post-compulsory disciplines.

Core responsibilities of the mentor role

As I have already indicated, each training institution will almost certainly set out in its own course-related documents the range of responsibilities (and sometimes entitlements) which mentors will have. Some of the possible specifications for mentors' activities – the requirements and boundaries of the role – are illustrated by the brief extracts from just one training scheme which are included below; clearly it is compliance with these which ought, ultimately, to inform how to approach working with a trainee. As would be evident from perusal of a larger sample, there are not huge variations in the ways in which mentoring is conceived by individual institutions; it would probably be somewhat puzzling if this were not found to be the case. Certain consistencies emerge, most of which are wholly concordant with those principles and practices advocated in the literature of mentoring. It is not, therefore, all that worthwhile to examine at any length what the numerous training institutions have specified, and the following 'snapshot' should suffice to give a flavour of current conceptions of the remit of mentors.

Cardiff University, when describing, for example, the purposes of regular mentor–trainee meetings, holds that these should be structured around opportunities to:

● discuss classroom experiences with a view to making teaching and learning more effective;

- focus on strategies to promote effective teaching and learning as appropriate to the subject;
- promote critical reflection on practice.

(Cardiff University 2003)

Mentors working in partnership with this particular scheme are advised to organise their meetings with trainees on a fortnightly basis. They are also advised that to complement their own observations of a trainee's developing practice they should liaise regarding further observations with those subject teachers being released from their normal class contact by virtue of groups being temporarily taught by trainees. (Thus the emerging requirements for additional observations can be complied with, as well as allowing a mentor to more effectively monitor classroom performance.)

Besides regular meetings and conducting observations, mentors attached to this scheme are typically also involved in:

- monitoring the lesson plans that trainees produce;
- writing reports and references;
- giving attention to the 'constraints and requirements' of such aspects of college life as external examinations;
- advising on the design and production of learning resources; and
- overseeing how trainees are planning to embed and develop key skills within their teaching.

(ibid.)

The mentoring 'mix'

Both from the above sample guidelines, and from various guidance provided later in this chapter, what may well become evident is the plain fact that mentoring college teachers encompasses not only providing certain wholly practical forms of assistance but some far less tangible, 'psychosocial' contributions to trainees' wellbeing and development. The mix may be said to be linked to the 'hard' and 'soft' skills, respectively, which are sometimes held to be involved in all professional life. Writing an observation report draws on the 'hard' skills of accurately reporting what went on in a class, and doing so within an acceptable time-frame and sensible word length. But it also requires the 'softer' skill of being able to imagine, and empathise with, the reader's response to the report – especially, of course, if it is one containing essential criticisms. Some mentoring activity will be most strongly dependent on mentors' 'hard' skills (including their subject-specific expertise), while at times their softer skills – their very nature or disposition – will come to the fore.

The mix of what is entailed in mentoring is apparent from the very earliest stage of a mentoring relationship with a new trainee. The new entrant to college teaching has a range of immediate practical needs, and will seek a mentor's help in meeting these – finding out what departmental resources are available is an obvious such *practical* issue. Other concerns of the new entrant may be far more *emotional* in origin and nature. Under this heading, there may well be quite pronounced, basic anxieties about survival:

> The survival theme has to do with reality shock, especially for teachers with no prior teaching experience, in confronting the complexity and simultaneity of instructional management: preoccupation with self ('Am I up to this challenge?'), the gulf between professional ideals and the daily grind of classroom life, the frag-mentation of tasks . . . the list goes on. (Huberman 1992: 123)

In other accounts of trainees' early preoccupations (e.g. Cunningham 2000) the fact that starting teaching is indeed a daunting transitional state is fairly evident, and interestingly, it seems almost unconnected with the maturity of the trainee. Recently (September 2004), a newly recruited trainee on a pre-service course wrote (anonymously): 'I'm very aware of how relatively young I am, and how much I still have to learn, and have trouble seeing myself as someone who has the authority/experience to teach.' Yet trainees with 20 or 30 years' industrial or commercial experience, and numerous accomplish-ments in their field, are not immune from their own distinctive concerns (including, notably, those concerning ageism), as witnessed by, for example, 'Can an old dog be taught new tricks [while] adapting it all to family life?' (ibid.).

Mentors will, therefore, be concerned with operating in various ways, prac-tical and otherwise, to ease the passage of trainees into a sector of education which has never previously presented quite such a range of professional oppor-tunities and challenges as it currently does. In such a context, it would perhaps be unsurprising if at times the litany of mentoring functions takes on a resem-blance to the 'lipsmackinthirstquenchin' Pepsi-Cola advertisement:

> teaching, coaching, advising, guiding, directing, protecting, supporting, sponsor-ing, challenging, encouraging, motivating, befriending, inspiring, *esteembuildin-rolemodellinformationgivinskillssharincareerdevelopinnovicenurturinrisk takingradeimprovinaspirationraisinhorizonbroadenintargetsettinkingmakinselfre-generatincriticallyreflectinperformanceassessinfeedbackgivin* . . .
> (Colley 2003: 31)

To avoid this blurring effect, however, what we must do is focus only on the specific actions – and their desired effects – which can feasibly be incorporated into the very restricted amount of regular contact between mentor and trainee which most 'real world' structures will allow for.

From their major survey of the mentoring literature, Johnson and Ridley (2004: xiv, xv) 'distilled' what they found into:

> 57 key *elements* for effective mentoring . . . clustered around six primary themes – what excellent mentors do (matters of skill); the traits of excellent mentors (matters of style and personality); arranging the mentor–protégé [sic] relationship (matters of beginning); knowing thyself as mentor (matters of integrity); when things go wrong (matters of restoration); and welcoming change and saying goodbye (matters of closure).

This 'further distillation' as we might term it, seems to be a useful one, succinctly encompassing *activity* and *chronology* as well as the *personal* and *interpersonal*.

Another attempt (and there have been many) to locate what exactly lies at the heart of effective mentoring was that of Anderson and Lucasse Shannon (1995: 29). They describe as the *essential attributes* of such mentoring:

> (a) the process of nurturing, (b) the act of serving as a role model, (c) the five mentoring functions (teaching, sponsoring, encouraging, counselling and befriending), (d) the focus on professional and personal development and (e) the ongoing caring relationship.

Particularly helpful are two *dispositions* which they also draw attention to, namely 'opening ourselves' and 'leading incrementally' (ibid.: 32). The latter notion encapsulates very well the idea that mentors cannot expect their work to be immediately transformative but must, most often, aim to be the overseers of a *gradual* process of a trainee's skills development.

However, closer, more specific *links* with our trainees and their professional sphere will still need to be made, which is the purpose of what follows. As noted earlier, much of the body of literature from which the foregoing samples have been extracted is not remotely concerned with PCET, yet we must aim to find ways in which mentoring will be most effective within this setting – drawing, where appropriate, on perspectives from other areas of professional activity when these do seem to have a real transferability.

Narrowing the focus

There is a set of core functions and responsibilities that can be specified for college-based mentors and which is, in some respects, timeless. By this I mean that no matter what the prevailing educational policies are, the nature of student cohorts or the stage we have reached in the development of available educational technologies, there exists an underlying set of trainee needs. Mentors will be involved in trying to meet these, whatever the externalities presented by an ever-changing educational environment are. By being attuned to the nature of the changes taking place, however, they will be able to deliver mentoring with modernity. The first specific function outlined below offers a good example of how, in a sense, the timelessness of certain needs can coexist with some of the wholly ephemeral, transitory aspects of present educational structures and systems, and in particular the discourse being generated by these.

Jargon-busting

For new (and 'newish') entrants to college teaching, one of the most daunting initial hurdles to overcome is that of becoming familiar with the enormous number of terms and abbreviations which post-compulsory education has spawned, especially since the early 1990s. It can be a dispiriting, excluding situation to be in a staffroom where social exchanges among experienced staff are dominated by language which is unlikely to be immediately accessible. College teaching, like all professional occupations, has what linguists would call its own 'sociolect'. This derives from such sources as:

- the range of descriptions applied to learner groups;
- curriculum policies and changes;
- other relevant legislation;
- college policies, procedures and documents; and
- subject-specific language, etc.

I have attempted to show in Figure 2.2 how we can sensibly view all this as essentially being related to certain 'scales', from the micro (i.e. individual students in their classrooms) to the macro (major social changes driving government policy). Each box of 'discourse', to borrow another term from sociolinguistics, nests inside a larger one. Illustrations of what may be found within each 'box' are then given

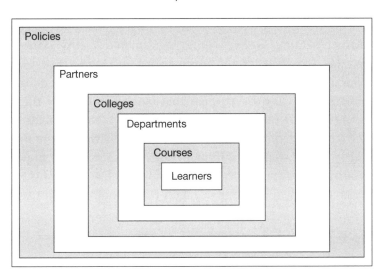

Figure 2.2 The sources of jargon in colleges

below. These, however, will almost certainly be supplemented during the life of this guide; some may become obsolete, and the current meanings attached to a further group will perhaps have changed. It seems, therefore, wisest to be thinking in terms of a changing inventory of terms, acronyms and abbreviations which in mentors' own judgement could usefully be explained as opportunities arise.

In this collation of sources of jargon, some illustrations of specific terms arising within each nesting box might include:

- **Learners**: Statemented; EMAs (education maintenance allowances); Link student; ALS (additional learning support), etc.

- **Courses**: Abbreviations relating to examination boards/awarding bodies; portfolios; criteria; specs (specifications), etc.

- **Departments**: Abbreviations relating to titles of these and key personnel within them such as HoD (head of department); 'Grade 2' (or other number) as a shorthand for departmental quality as judged by OfSTED, etc.

- **Colleges**: Abbreviations relating to key personnel such as VP (vice principal); site names where a college is 'split site'; terms used to designate special functions of parts of the premises – 'help desk'; SAR (self-assessment report), etc.

- **Partners**: LSC (Learning and Skills Council); governors; names/abbreviations for institutions with which franchising arrangements exist; OfSTED, etc.

- **Policies**; Tomlinson (referring to the implementation plans triggered by the Report); Kennedy (referring to the widening participation policies arising from the Report); MAs (modern apprenticeships), etc.

What is clearly essential, just as it would be in mentors' own classrooms, is to promote an ethos in which 'it's OK not to know', and saying 'just ask if there's anything which doesn't make sense' is an integral part of the mentoring repertoire. Mentors should reassure trainees that being bemused by the jargon of college life, the evolving qualifications structure etc., is not an inadequacy, and is something which can quite speedily – almost always well before the end of a PGCE/CertEd – be got over. It is, though, hard to overstate the importance of inducting trainees into this aspect of the professional world that is the college sector today, to enhance the confidence with which they will approach it.

Inducting trainees into the 'broader themes'

Being provided with the right language ('PCET-speak') is, of course, only one side of the equation; the major concerns and preoccupations of the college sector have an actuality which impacts on new teachers from their first day in the job. Trainees are, of course, taught about a range of such concerns during the PGCE/CertEd programmes they attend. (At the time of writing this is being done by training institutions to comply with coverage of FENTO/LLUK's statements under the heading of 'Domain-wide knowledge and critical understanding'.)

However, there can be no really adequate substitute for direct encounters with certain issues, and dialogue with informed mentors about these. We could probably each identify what we conceive of as some of the present 'really big issues' in the sector, and there would no doubt be a fairly high degree of overlap between what one practitioner sees as being of major importance and what another would highlight. There could well be a consensus that understanding all of the following developments, so that we can most effectively respond to the challenges they present, is essential:

Table 2.1 *Recent changes in post-compulsory education*

● Widening participation
● The nature of inspection
● Shifts in interest away from 16+ and towards 14+ transitions
● Far greater attention given to inclusion/additional learning needs
● Growth in student entitlements
● Focus on individual learning and achievement rather than on groups
● 'Quality'-related initiatives and the growth of an audit culture
● The prime importance of student retention
● Competition between education providers in a 'marketised' local environment
● The expanded professional roles and responsibilities of teachers
● Overriding management anxieties regarding funding allocations

The listing is, as I acknowledge, one that might not be exactly replicated by other observers of recent changes in the post-compulsory sector, but any variations might not be too startling. It is quite possible that some would add to the list such other discrete items as key skills, coursework and e-learning. On the other hand, if we really do start to see more of the promised local collaborative, e.g. consortium-type, arrangements among providers than exist at present, then the 'competition' item could be deleted.

It would be hard, and probably unnecessary, in a guide of this length to detail the implications of every issue proposed here as being of significance, and to describe for each one a set of strategies which mentors might adopt to allow trainees to more easily make connections between the developments and their own experiences. But it is the business of *making links* between the items in the list and the placement or employing college which is important, not making an attempt to 'begin at square one' and, in didactic fashion, lecture trainees (which will be happening elsewhere). For the present, illustrations of how mentors may guide and support their trainees in one or two areas might, however, be of value:

- *Student entitlements:* Developments in this area do, of course, *visibly* connect with what has been witnessed in at least two others: increased competition for students since the early 1990s and the recent importance attached to debates over colleges' ability to retain students once they are recruited. There are, no doubt, strongly altruistic elements involved in a drive to ensure that students are getting a fair deal from a college and from their teachers in particular; it would be deeply cynical to fail to recognise this. Yet it is only balanced to suggest that colleges need to ensure that entitlements are met so that the potential for withdrawal, complaint or litigation is greatly minimised. No college could afford the damaging effects on its local reputation that would result from a publicised complaint about a failure on its part to meet a student's entitlement, or to provide a 'quality learning experience'.

At a basic level mentors can simply provide trainees with whatever documents or statements are supplied to students in which their entitlements are set out (some of which are perhaps not otherwise going to be supplied to teachers). They can provide additional guidance on the nature of the 'constructive formative feedback' that such documents usually promise students. They can, similarly, exemplify what was meant within the institution when a statement relating to 'regular individual tutorials' was framed. They can very strongly promote in trainees the merits of encouraging their learners always to raise any concerns with them before reporting them in other quarters. And, in worst-case scenarios, they may offer to intervene/act as mediator should an 'entitlement' issue between a trainee/learner (or learner group) not appear to be susceptible to a straightforward resolution. (Sometimes, if this stage is reached, it may emerge that a particular student has been falling down with regard to *their responsibilities* alongside claiming entitlements having been unmet.) Overarching all of these possible actions, though, there is, yet again, the need to ensure clarity regarding the rationale for student entitlements and to display a positive attitude towards this aspect of the current educational scene.

- *Quality and audit:* It would quite easily be possible to write a book-length review of issues under this heading. There is often a marked degree of negativity flavouring discussions of quality assurance, procedures such as 'internal review/audit' and the very much greater emphasis being placed by managers on teachers' compliance with requests for various forms of student- and course-related data. The terms 'paperchase' and 'paper trail' have become fairly commonplace, and the proposition that teachers sometimes seem to spend as much time documenting their teaching as actually teaching is encountered in not a few staffrooms. In my own experience, both trainees and recently qualified new teachers perceive the whole area as being, in general, daunting and demotivating. 'I don't think anyone ever reads any of the stuff anyway' is the kind of sentiment quite routinely expressed concerning much of the documentation which must be supplied in the name of quality assurance.

So, how much of value can mentors hope to bring to such a situation? There appear to be both 'philosophical' and practical inputs that might be supportive ones for trainees. In terms of the former, it may for example be very worthwhile pointing to the available evidence relating to retention and achievement: although there are pockets of poor performance in the sector, some colleges are performing very well indeed, and *overall* (in terms of numbers of students achieving their target qualifications), results have been steadily improving (Kingston 2004). While we could not legitimately attribute all of this improvement to closer scrutiny of teachers' work, and more rigorous, in-depth QA procedures, some elements of it have very probably derived from the more prominent position that 'quality' now occupies on most colleges' agendas. Close monitoring of results across curriculum areas has allowed for additional resourcing, and targeted support for the professional development of staff. The use of value added analysis, and benchmarking (just two of the tools now available to us when researching quality issues) has indicated areas where achievement levels are not concomitant with what might be expected of a cohort. To veer into a discussion of retention, the much greater efforts put into finding out why students are expressing dissatisfaction or withdrawing have similarly allowed us to put together a picture of where exactly we need to be cranking up levels of support, or improving teaching quality.

These kinds of things can be presented as positives, as can – at a more practical level – the merits of maintaining up-to-date schemes of work, full records for individual students and so on: the sorts of data virtually all colleges' QA systems will require. Compiling a bank of lesson plans seems especially easy to justify to trainees as being worth the effort expended: such a resource ultimately becomes an investment, and an eminently transferable one at that – with the necessary updating it might well serve a teacher well in a subsequent post. The sheer professionality of having taken the time to properly design learning sessions should be promoted, as well as the sense of security which can come from teaching a, perhaps challenging, group on the basis of a sound set of learning objectives/timings/activities having been clearly laid out, rather than relying on the 'note on the back of an envelope' approach. Mentors perform an especially valuable service for trainees when they take an interest in their developing planning skills, and praise any strong efforts in this area that they notice.

What mentors are actually doing when engaging in dialogue on these issues (and providing assistance in practical ways) is *accelerating* the professional learning of their trainees. As noted elsewhere in this guide, training programmes are brief and can offer but a 'precis' of some of the key features of the PCET environment; to more speedily and confidently be able to appreciate these fully, trainees will, far more often than not, benefit from a mentor's targeted inputs.

Day-to-day realities

In some ways, it is possible to conceive of a 'mentoring *syllabus*' comprising both coverage of the kinds of issues outlined above (focusing in particular on how they are impacting locally) and many other far less weighty, but nevertheless important, matters (see below). The notion of a syllabus might seem to contradict what was put forward in the Introduction – that mentoring as a professional activity is far from mechanical and should be informed by discretion. But it would only be mechanistic if an absolutely rigid, inflexible chronology and sequencing of 'topics' were to be proposed. Quite obviously, some items will need to be dealt with at a much earlier stage than others. But beyond making this point it is probably true that each individual trainee's 'need to know' will be different. It is probably, in the above context, to record what has been discussed at each of the regular meetings (probably weekly) which mentors will hold with their trainees – what ground has been covered, and how it is proposed to follow this up. Here, incidentally, is one of the numerous ways in which mentoring or supervision meetings might be likened to the individual tutorials we run with learners (where these are based on their individual learning plans, rather than being events triggered by personal crises of one form or another, or, say, infringements of disciplinary codes).

Other key dimensions of the mentoring role which are therefore worth underlining include addressing certain practical considerations which may seem entirely mundane – banal even – but which have a very strong impact on the ease with which trainees can acclimatise to college life. It is probably artificial to attempt to intellectualise about the kinds of practicalities dealt with in this section, beyond saying that we will be promoting the development of the kind of confident 'artisanry' which flourishes 'when things go well, when the routines work smoothly [leading to] a rush of craft pride that translates into what has come to be called "self-efficacy"' (Huberman 1992: 136).

A mentoring 'toolkit'?

Although much of what follows will clearly relate mostly to trainees on pre-service courses, or to new appointees, we do need to be confident that a range of essentials to do with 'housekeeping' and college procedures is dealt with. In certain respects, to borrow an idea from Napper and Batchelor (1989), dealing with these is most efficiently accomplished where mentors have organised for themselves a 'toolkit' of aids. The contents of this would differ from college to college, and between curriculum areas, but it might well include:

- a staff handbook;
- a student handbook;
- a package of exam board specifications relating to the courses offered within the relevant curriculum area;
- samples of past question papers and/or project briefs;
- summary notes relating to available departmental resources;
- any group or individual learner profiles which have been produced (although trainees usually have to produce these for themselves, to comply with one course assessment or another);
- guidance on the all-important photocopying (see below);
- master key where appropriate.

Mentors should have been supplied with such items as a handbook for the specific training course being followed, with key reporting documents either contained within this or provided separately; such an item constitutes essential reference material for the mentor as opposed to those in the list above, which clearly are for sharing with the trainee.

It is also important that mentors make explicit to trainees (that is, those not actually employed by a college) that registers and various other documents essential for college administration have to be dealt with alongside 'just teaching'. These are vital pieces of paperwork, not only for funding reasons, of course, but, for example, in connection with monitoring student performance where individuals are 'on report'. It is wise to prepare trainees for the kinds of situations where students will approach them with attendance slips for signature, and so on. The use of electronic registers has caused problems for not a few trainees, and it would be wrong to assume that everyone will find these completely straightforward.

Some other particularly frequently encountered issues, for which possession of a 'toolkit' may be a useful basis for action, are set out below.

Photocopying issues

Trainees may well not have an unambiguous view of what it is, or is not, legitimate to request under the heading of *teaching resources*. The photocopied handout remains such a staple of our learning resources mix that photocopying always seems to throw up a number of problems. Each college will have its own arrangements for dispensing photocopying entitlements, for instance, and questions arising from this, absolutely crucial, issue might include:

- What is the maximum number of photocopies for my classes I can have per term?
- Do I need my own personal card/code to make use of the copier?
- Must I record anywhere the number of copies I am making?
- If I make too many copies does this reduce the total available for other members of the department?
- What are the arrangements regarding paper for the copier if the supply runs out while I am using it (and can I legitimately request help with loading this if I run into difficulties)?
- Am I allowed to use existing stocks of photocopied sheets in a departmental resources bank, and if so, must I assume responsibility for replacing these?
- What is the right kind of film to feed through the copier when I want to make transparencies? (This almost merits its own 'lesson', given the expense and inconvenience to an institution caused by the wrong – incompatible – transparency film for a particular copier being used.)

As with many other such apparently trivial questions, even the half-dozen or so above does not exhaust the range of possible queries.

These kinds of matters are ones which, of course, will not usually stretch mentors' knowledge and awareness of what is 'correct' in the context of a specific institution. While it may appear tedious to deal with them, this possibility is, however, offset by the smoothness with which practicalities will become non-problematic for trainees.

Keys to rooms

All educational institutions have necessarily become greatly more security conscious in recent years, with the use of ID and swipe cards becoming commonplace, for example, and much more emphasis on the need to 'please keep doors locked when rooms are unoccupied'. Most college staff, and legitimate visitors, have few, if any, criticisms of this trend – though they may of course lament the circumstances which have given rise to it. For a trainee, especially one on a pre-service course and therefore not having employed status, special problems may arise, however, particularly with regard to keys.

We all promote the kind of professionalism signalled by arriving early at the room in which a class is to be taught, allowing for any sensible rearrangements of furniture, checking of OHPs, etc. before a lesson. If rooms are in continuous use – i.e. one group leaving as another enters – then the problem of having to locate keys does not arise. However, if trainees will regularly be teaching in rooms that have been locked for security, then they really do need to either be provided with keys or know where exactly they can be accessed or borrowed. This is one of those apparently very minor issues but is one of real significance. Relations between trainees and their groups can be quite adversely affected by the kind of 'messy' start to a lesson which not being able to get into a classroom often results in. If on eventually getting into a room it is found to need substantial tidying up then this can lead to a situation, especially with more challenging young groups, where an unsettled, perhaps noisy, start can breed further disruption. (And a room simply *left* littered and/or with its furniture all over the place really is not a conducive learning environment.) At the very least, given the reduced course hours syndrome which has been witnessed, the amount of time lost from teaching can be a cause for concern.

To make for a smoother experience for both trainee and learners, the availability of keys is, then, an important consideration. For the pre-service trainee it can add to their sense of belonging to have their own key; one element of being 'not just a student'.

OHT projector bulbs, VCR remote control handsets, etc.

These small items can also cause a large amount of needless stress when they are broken or have gone missing. Well-organised, generously resourced, college departments might have the services of dedicated support staff monitoring the availability and serviceability of such items, but this situation is probably quite rare. Mentors can perform such supportive tasks as demonstrating to trainees how a spare bulb is activated in the kind of projector that has a lever to bring it into use after one has failed. They might mark, with 'Tippex' for example, the room number in which a 'remote' should remain. Far more importantly, though, they should take as a guiding principle that trainees will generally be grateful for, rather than patronised by, the offer of pointers and assistance in connection with some of the basic technology of classrooms.

Most trainers and observers of teaching will have witnessed the distraction and sometimes real distress which trainees can experience when thwarted, in front of a group of learners, by 'simple' things. Anything we can do to militate against this is time well spent.

Flipchart holders/pages

This is another very 'basic' matter that has the potential to cause a quite disproportionate degree of inconvenience if overlooked. A1-sized flipchart pads remain in frequent use in classrooms, sometimes in fairly wasteful use (single words or book titles filling up a page, and so on). It can be a very rapid process indeed to use up a pad. With some classroom activities, groupwork especially, calling for the results of activities to be summarised by students on flipchart sheets, this tendency can be exacerbated.

Besides taking the obvious step of pointing out the need for a measure of economy – flipchart pads are surprisingly expensive – mentors can usefully ensure that the location of replacement pads is known, because almost certainly the question will arise. If a department allows or encourages the products of student work to be attached to classroom walls, another common request which can be pre-empted is for Blu-Tack™ so that this can easily be done.

The 'right kind' of pen

It is particularly easy to take for granted that trainees will know which pen/marker is correct for which medium/surface. We do, though, usually need to spend some time running through the importance to a trainee of checking the labels on pens, as well as letting them know where to find what they need. The various widths of OHT marker pen (from Superfine (SF) to Broad (B)) are worth indicating, as is the fact that they can be bought in both water-based and permanent variants – both of which have their uses.

Whiteboards can be quite seriously damaged by use of markers other than the 'dry-wipe' kind, and the ill will this can generate among colleagues is worth noting. Trainees need some succinct advice on what to do if the board in their classroom has – usually in spite of a large warning notice – been written on with a fluid, proving hard, if not impossible, to remove. If no flipchart holder/paper is available as an alternative, this kind of thing can cause much irritation and stress.

'Can I move the room around?'

In certain teaching contexts – the laboratory, say, or the computer suite – there are extremely limited opportunities for room rearrangements. (It may sometimes be possible and desirable to ask learners to move their wheeled chairs away from computer workstations and towards the front of the room to listen to short, whole-group explanations.) In most non-specialist classrooms, however, for sound pedagogic reasons, we might want to encourage trainees to adapt room layouts for specific types of lessons. Discussion/seminar work is obviously best conducted with 'horseshoe' or semicircular seating arrangements, to facilitate eye contact – seeing which member of a group is making a point, etc. The 'committee' layout is said to work best for whole-group simulations, and 'café-style' for small group or pairwork. And largely didactic sessions, or ones including a high proportion of individual work on tasks, can happily be run using the traditional 'rows' layout.

What is self-evident, based on the results of very many observations of practical teaching, is that a mismatch between room layout and the nature and purpose of teaching is a recipe for disaster. It is nearly always best if room rearrangements are allowed, but for the sake of goodwill we must stress the importance of returning classrooms to the layout in which they were found. Teachers with 'majority use' of a classroom can be especially affronted by temporary, unwanted rearrangements and their position should be properly considered. Similarly, we should always encourage trainees to try to ensure that their learners don't leave too much debris in rooms for others to deal with – another potential source of discord which is fairly easily avoided. These kinds of areas may, I acknowledge, appear to be entirely trivial from certain perspectives, yet a reference request on my desk at the time of writing, from a high-profile sixth-form college, asks for my comment on whether a candidate for a post 'keeps areas tidy and attractive'. The orderliness of learning environments is surely a motivating factor both for teachers *and* their learners.

Arrangements to do with accompanying or leading educational visits

It is, of course, a very valuable part of a trainee's experience to be involved with curriculum-related trips, and purely 'social' ones involving groups of students. For reasons strongly associated with a number of tragic mishaps that have occurred on recent school or college trips (and the almost inevitable litigation which has ensued), all PCET institutions now need to be much more aware of their responsibilities with regard to such matters as:

- staff–student ratios when off the premises;
- appropriate certification (first aid, approval for minibus use, etc.);
- parental permission in respect of 14–19 learners; and
- procedures in connection with expenses incurred.

In general, agreeing to a trainee on a pre-service course assuming prime responsibility for planning and leading an educational visit is not to be recommended. Trainees who are employed by a college need to be especially fully cognisant with the contents of the institution's *risk assessment* procedures, given their contractual obligations to comply with such published guidelines.

Trainees and learning materials

All trainees will need to be guided and supported in matters to do with the core function of being able to 'select and develop resources to support learning' (FENTO 2000, 'Key area of teaching', d5). In the real world of most college settings, this activity will generally include a very significant focus on text-based materials – handouts and worksheets in particular. Mentors will be serving trainees' interests well if they, first, encourage experimentation with such materials; this is especially so as the great majority of training providers will be seeking evidence in their trainees of an independent and creative approach to designing materials.

Clearly, however, it will not be advisable to promote the use of newly designed materials without these first having been commented on by mentors. As with many aspects of the mentoring relationship, we are not advocating any kind of 'vetting' of trainees' performance in an area of teaching, rather the provision of *opportunities* for the discussion of, in this case, printed materials being proposed for use with a learner group. Perhaps most importantly, mentors can use their experience and insights to:

- advise on whether the language level adopted on a sample of material is well aligned with the linguistic abilities of the group for whom it is intended. Might a glossary of topic-specific terms be a valuable addition to a handout, for instance? Are sentence constructions over-long? Is the phrasing of any of the questions/instructions ambiguous? (an extremely common fault seen in a high proportion of early attempts made by trainees);

- tactfully point out spelling and grammatical errors (which learners will more often than not tend to reproduce in their own work) and reiterate what is sadly true, that computer spellchecks cannot ever identify all of these;

- make useful suggestions for promoting interactive use of the materials: what must learners actually *do* with what they will be provided with, beyond simply filing it? Have useful exercises been suggested, are there gaps in information which will require learners to usefully engage in research (or other activity) so that these can be filled in? Are there any pointers to further reading? Has the material been set in context, i.e. connected in some way to a specific part of a course?

Mentors will, of course, be highly aware of the time constraints under which teachers have to work, and will know well the merits of 'not reinventing the wheel'. Therefore, encouraging trainees to scrutinise materials to see whether they might be *amended, adapted, refined or updated* is both sensible and supportive. All trainees will be required to demonstrate that they can devise original materials, but in reality, doing so ought to be paralled by using their developing judgement to select items which, if less than ideal in their present form, can be made to mesh with the needs of particular learner groups.

Where there is a group of trainees based in an institution, it could be productive to elicit what support there might be for a learning materials 'exhibition'. At such an event, trainees could, in turn, display and describe an aid they are using, reviewing the ways in which it might be claimed to be enhancing student learning. The rationale for opting for a particular format (e.g. OHT rather than handout) can be provided, and pointers provided as to how the aid might be supplemented or further developed. What tends to emerge in such a forum is that trainees from other specialisms (stimulated by the right kind of questioning from a skilled facilitator) discern how the value of particular aids is frequently not exclusive to one domain – with the kind of adaptation and refinement proposed above they will often be useful more widely.

Awareness of employment-related issues

A sometimes overlooked dimension of mentoring is the value of keeping up to date with what kinds of requirements are being expressed by the PCET sector regarding candidates for teaching posts. I am not implying in what follows that mentors should aspire to become careers advisers, but being able to transmit to trainees 'really useful knowledge' about the realities of employment in the sector is often much appreciated. Of course, trainees can research for themselves what kinds of skills and experience are being sought (by using college websites and simply sending for applicant packs/post descriptions when jobs are advertised). Whether mentors can offer something over and above this lies in their being able to *facilitate the gaining of appropriate experience*. This dimension of the experiential learning being designed for a trainee is one that focuses on a broader range of dispositions and competences than those exclusively associated with classroom teaching.

To illustrate what is meant, it is evident that employers are increasingly being explicit regarding such things as:

- the ability to write reports;
- being able to provide consultation for students, their parents and other parties;
- personal tutorial responsibilities;
- teamworking;
- being up to date with policy and curriculum developments and with professional standards in the area of attendance.

While it would probably be unnecessary to point out what exactly mentors should do regarding each of these in turn (and a much longer list would be possible – that above is merely a sample based on what one sixth-form college was recently highlighting), one or two indications may be of value. Regarding *tutoring*, for example, mentors might allow access to at least their own group tutorial sessions, so that the operation of a tutorial curriculum might be observed at first hand. And, provided consent is given by the learner, some individual tutorial work might be sat in on, for instance where a progress review is being conducted. Many trainees (certainly this holds true for those on pre-service courses) will not be given a tutorial role; to an extent, this fact can disadvantage them when seeking first posts. Any opportunity to see what this crucial part of professional activity in PCET entails will be worthwhile. Similarly, facilitating and strongly encouraging attendance – and, even better, participation – by trainees at 'open evenings' and other such events is sensible. At these, parents and prospective students are given advice as to what the options might be within an institution, and witnessing this process is to be recommended. Trainees benefit not only from seeing this at work but also from exposure to an even more diverse mix of individuals than those in their classes.

These kinds of things broaden trainees' understanding of the *raison d'être* of the sector, and will undoubtedly allow them to construct more convincing CVs when applying for posts. In some senses, what mentors can accomplish here on behalf of their trainees has as much to commend it as being able to volunteer to do things such as read drafts of supporting statements and/or provide references in connection with applications.

One important dimension of the current employment scene, of which mentors may perhaps not have an overview, is the importance being attached to such matters as *reliability* – indeed from the numerous reference requests I receive it almost seems appropriate to describe employability as hinging on 'reliability, reliability, reliability'. Employer requests to specify exact percentages of actual/possible attendances by a trainee are not uncommon, and the same kind of thing applies to punctuality. Mentors would be doing trainees a disservice by not raising their awareness of such realities.

Ultimately, even though the kinds of commitments mentors would offer in these areas are unlikely to be specified as *entitlements* for trainees, they can play an extremely useful part in the socialisation process often viewed as an important strand within mentoring relationships. Self-awareness on mentors' parts regarding what *they themselves* feel they would have liked to be 'taught' (as opposed to having simply 'caught') early on in their careers can play as useful a role in informing what 'non-classroom' opportunities are set up for trainees as perusing what colleges are seeking in new entrants.

'What do mentors *not* need to do?'

It is perhaps surprising to find the inclusion in this guide of a section titled in this way. However, there are a number of components of an initial teacher training programme for which clear responsibility rests with trainers/tutors rather than mentors. There is an essential division of labour that is required for the successful delivery of such programmes because (remembering the short time period involved) no single individual can cover every essential. Trainers – often, but not exclusively, based in universities – are best placed to deal with certain things, while practising college-based subject specialists are the right people to lead trainees' professional learning relating to other things, some obvious examples being their specialisms, their associated pedagogy, exam board specifications and the local arrangements and constraints affecting learning and teaching.

It is entirely legitimate that mentors hold certain expectations regarding what their trainees should know and can do on the basis of their attending an endorsed PCET training course. Were this not to hold true, mentors would simply be overwhelmed by the quantity of information and the nature of some of the principles and concepts they might be expected to impart to trainees (which is *not* to imply that mentors would in any way be intellectually challenged by much of the generic material covered by trainers; there are certainly issues over the greater, more convenient, accessibility for trainers of certain learning- and teaching-related resources and the availability to universities of speakers who are experts in various policy or practice domains, but the point being made here primarily relates to volume – to quantity rather than to quality).

To allow for a more efficient concentration of their time and energies, mentors, in general, would be advised not to attempt to deal, on a 'from square one' basis, with such issues as:

- the *basics* of lesson planning (the nature of aims/objectives; the need to provide timings for lesson segments; the need to demonstrate variety of learner activities, etc.);
- a *general* review of the principal learning resources available to teachers (the various boards; video; OHPs);
- trying to encapsulate the major features of the present landscape of educational policy, or the funding of PCET institutions – areas which are covered as a result of the FENTO/LLUK stipulations regarding trainers' needs to acquire 'domain-wide knowledge and critical understanding' of 'the place of FE within the wider context', 'current national and international initiatives' and 'sources of funding';

- the continuing debates, and disagreements, over inclusivity, differentiation and learning styles, which are being given some prominence on virtually all training programmes.

These are the kinds of techniques, principles and policies that any self-respecting training programme ought to have adequately addressed. Some – most especially those falling under the heading of 'techniques' – may well need, over time, to be *revisited* by mentors, but there is no great profit in starting from an assumption of nil knowledge, and nor is there the time which would be needed to do so. Clearly, whether or not a trainee has encountered a particular issue, or topic, will depend on the stage they are at on their training programme. (One supplement to the kind of mentors' 'toolkit' proposed in this guide could be a copy of the training institution's taught programme, so that it can be ascertained whether something has or has not been dealt with.)

The kind of listing shown above can only ever exemplify what the individual trainee's experience has been. Notwithstanding the ostensibly standardised nature of accredited training programmes, certain variations do exist – in emphasis more often than in actual content. For this reason there is value in at least looking at what is contained in the trainee's particular course handbook, and preferably clarifying anything that is not clear with the trainee him/herself. Mentors' prime role in connection with the kinds of practical/policy issues being addressed by trainers becomes one of facilitating a set of *connections* between these and the local opportunities and constraints that trainees will encounter in a specific institution.

For example, in connection with such important recent legislation as the Disability Discrimination Act (DDA) (1995), what will be of special relevance for trainees is the set of responses that has been made to this. How has the college refined its selection procedures (for both students and staff) in line with the DDA? What physical adaptations to the premises have had to be made? Have any significant adjustments been made to support and guidance structures and – most importantly from a trainee's perspective – to the kinds of pedagogies being promoted in the college?

With regard to developments connected to the 14–19 agenda, the sorts of questions that might be addressed were perhaps hinted at recently by Ruth Silver in one of the numerous articles that collectively formed a kind of 'inquest' on the failure of the Tomlinson Committee Report to achieve all its aims. Her view was that a 14–19 solution will comprise far more than 'beefing up existing collaborative initiatives such as the government's "increased flexibility" programme, under which 14-year-olds disaffected at school can spend a day a week in colleges pursuing more vocational activities':

There are currently about 100,000 school pupils studying in further education. The future won't simply be more of the same . . . If we really want 14 to 19 reform, that won't be enough. (Ruth Silver, in Kingston 2005)

What a mentor might be raising a trainee's awareness of is, therefore, the current scale of 14–19 provision within the particular institution, how successful it is deemed to have been and what plans are emerging to refine what is on offer in the light of concerns such as those illustrated above. The example of 14–19 developments is chosen here because, in my experience, the whole debate is one which does appear to unsettle a number of trainees, for reasons hinted at in the same article:

> But wouldn't the wholesale migration of 14-year-olds into the essentially adult atmosphere of colleges pose too many problems? 'Full-time 14-year-olds in colleges bring all sorts of legal implications of in loco parentis and child protection,' says Norman Lucas, director of post-compulsory teacher education at London University's Institute of Education. 'Then you've got the "kiddification" of FE. If you've got hordes of 14-year-olds full-time, the implication is the opposite of the open atmosphere you want for adult education.' (ibid.)

The high value of mentors' work here lies, as I have indicated, in filling in all the *local details* of a national picture which can only ever have been given the 'broad brush' treatment by a training institution, as it will have been in much of the contemporary literature. What is entailed is clearly having an informed grasp of what is taking place outside the confines of a specific curriculum department, at different scales and organisational levels within an institution. It may be that one component of such awareness-raising as I have advocated will be liaising with key personnel to obtain from them relevant materials – and possibly even their agreement to talk informally with a trainee regarding 'work in progress' – to meet the requirements of national educational policy.

References

Anderson, E. M. and Lucasse Shannon, A. (1995) 'Towards a conceptualisation of mentoring', in Kerry, T. and Shelton Mayes, A. (eds) *Issues in Mentoring*. London: Routledge.

Cardiff University (2003) Teaching Practice Guide for Students, Mentors and Link Tutors. Cardiff: Cardiff University School of Social Sciences.

Carr, D. (1992) 'Four dimensions of educational professionalism'. *Westminster Studies in Education*, 15, 19–31.

Colley, H. (2003) *Mentoring for Social Inclusion: A Critical Approach to Nurturing Mentor Relationships*. London: RoutledgeFalmer.

Cunningham, B. (2000) 'Beginning close encounters: on starting to teach in colleges'. *Teacher Development*, 4 (3), 241–56.

DfES (2004) *Equipping Our Teachers for the Future: Reforming Initial Teacher Training for the Learning and Skills Sector*. Nottingham: Department for Education and Skills.

Disability Discrimination Act (1995). London: The Stationery Office.

FENTO (2000) *Standards for Teaching and Supporting Learning in England and Wales*. London: Further Education National Training Organisation.

FENTO (2001) *Mentoring Towards Excellence*. London: Further Education National Training Organisation.

Fry, H., Ketteridge, S. and Marshall, S. (1999) *A Handbook for Teaching and Learning in Higher Education: Enhancing Academic Practice*. London: Kogan Page.

Hargreaves, A. and Fullan, M. G. (1992) *Understanding Teacher Development*. New York: Teachers College Press.

Healy, C. C. and Welchert, A. J. (1990) 'Mentoring relations: a definition to advance research and practice'. *Educational Researcher*, **19**(9), 17–21.

Hoyle, E. (1974) 'Professionality, professionalism and control in teaching'. *London Education Review*, **3**(2).

Huberman, M. (1992) 'Teacher development and instructional mastery', in Hargreaves, A. and Fullan, M. G. *Understanding Teacher Development*. New York: Teachers College Press.

Huddleston, P. and Unwin, L. (2002) *Teaching and Learning in Further Education* (2nd edn). London: RoutledgeFalmer.

Jackson, P. W. (1992) 'Helping teachers develop', in Hargreaves, A. and Fullan, M. G. *Understanding Teacher Development*. New York: Teachers College Press.

Johnson, W. B. and Ridley, C. R. (2004) *The Elements of Mentoring*. New York: Palgrave Macmillan.

Kingston, P. (2004) 'More colleges fail in south'. *Education Guardian*, 30 November.

Kingston, P. (2005) 'Opportunity knocks'. *The Guardian*, 22 February.

Napper, R. and Batchelor, D. (1989) *A Tutor's Toolkit: An Open Learning Resource for First Time Tutors*. Cambridge: National Extension College.

Sachs, J. (2001) 'Teacher professional identity: competing discourses, competing outcomes'. *Journal of Education Policy*, **16**(2), 149–61.

Waterhouse, P. (1991) *Tutoring*. Stafford: Network Educational.

Mentoring and models of professional learning

Chapter objective:

- To enable mentors to confidently underpin their practice by being able to draw on selected models of professional learning.

How feasible are the aspirations of those who hope to codify teachers' craft knowledge? It is not difficult to find maxims or practical tips to pass on to beginning teachers, but what do they all add up to? . . . Can an amorphous collection of practical principles be said to constitute a grounded theory of practice, or is this mere wishful thinking? (Eraut 1994)

Practice without a grounding of theory is likely to be sterile at best, and ineffective and damaging at worst. Being sent straight into the classroom for a large block of time without a chance of reflection is not the best way.
(from a letter titled 'Real teacher training', *Education Guardian*, 22 March 2005)

It is hoped that at least some exposure to an albeit quite limited range of theory (in the form of selected models of professionalism and professional learning) will add both interest and insight to the activity of mentoring. As with all professional work worthy of the description, mentoring is not merely concerned with practicalities and a mechanistic, rule-bound approach to tasks. Some cognisance of broader, conceptual frameworks which might underpin the activity is very worthwhile, if not actually essential. To this end I will therefore select a small number of theoretical perspectives that, it appears, can profitably *be applied* to the process of understanding the contribution that effective mentoring might make to the early professional development of PCET teachers; it needs to be stressed, however, that the models are only being presented in skeletal form, and that none is derived specifically from research in our sector.

In their 1995 paper on the training of college teachers, Young *et al.* (1995) referred to the 'benign neglect' which they saw as having long afflicted the post-compulsory sector. One of the ways in which this was evident was to be found in a real dearth of literature devoted to professional issues in the PCET sector. This observation is one contrasting strongly with what has long been available, with a focus on school teaching. To a large extent, not a great deal has changed over the past decade or so: a high proportion of what is published on *professional*, as opposed to *policy*, issues is still originating in work focused on phases of education other than PCET. It is for this reason that the reader will find so little here based on researching college teachers. And certain of the perspectives apply more strongly to 'learning *teaching*' than to 'learning *mentoring*', but, as I hope will be evident, trying to draw a line between these two types of professional learning may be neither straightforward nor productive.

'Artisanry' and the learning of a craft

The notion of teaching as a craft skill is an interesting one, which has been particularly thoughtfully examined by Michael Huberman. Although his exposition of the 'craft' model makes no explicit reference to mentoring, we can see without too much difficulty where a skilled mentor could play a crucial role.

Essentially, teachers are artisans working primarily alone, with a variety of new and cobbled-together materials, in a personally designed work environment. They gradually develop a repertoire of instructional skills and strategies, corresponding to a progressively denser, more differentiated and well-integrated set of mental schemata. They come to read the instructional situation better and faster, and to respond to it with a greater variety of tools. They develop this repertoire through a somewhat haphazard process of trial and error, usually when one or another segment of the repertoire does not work repeatedly. Somewhere in that cycle '*they may reach out to peers or . . . professional trainers* [and] transform those inputs into a more private, personally congenial form' (Huberman 1992: 136, emphasis added).

For 'peers or . . . professional trainers' I would claim that it is now entirely legitimate to substitute 'mentors'; after all, in the specific US educational context that Huberman had in mind (certainly at the time he was observing its key features), the role of formal mentors would have been minuscule. The point that can surely be emphasised is that mentoring allows for far more *active* interventions than are alluded to above, where inputs are obtained purely on the basis of a 'reaching out' by someone in the process of developing their craft skills. Effective mentors can potentially initiate an *acceleration* of trainees' professional learning in a context where they are not simply passive until such a time as they are reached out to. This is not to negate the significance of trial-and-error learning. The importance of this has been highlighted by other writers such as David Hargreaves: 'mentors' regular inputs will productively complement this, not replace it. They will, by encouraging open discussion of the "errors" – the things which "[do] not work repeatedly" – deepen trainees' understanding of these, and can engage in reviewing possible alternative strategies, or "tools" in Huberman's phrasing (Hargreaves 1999).

What will be an essential precondition for the above formulation to be a credible one will obviously be the degree to which a mentor (and/or a department) has explicitly allowed a trainee 'the freedom to fail'. This hinges on the key question of whether a trainee will be fearful of the consequences of owning up to mistakes, or will feel secure and comfortable in doing so. As one trainee put it: 'Making us feel that no mistake is disastrous would be great' (FT, pre-service trainee, 2004). But such a consideration applies, of course, to many of the models relating to professional learning, and certainly to most of those which will comprise the rest of the present brief review.

Learning through reflection on experience

Experiential learning is probably the one single theoretical perspective likely to be of special utility to mentors. The term is perhaps most frequently associated with the work of Kolb (1984), although there are a number of other writers – both before and after Kolb – who examine the key dimensions of learning from experience. Dennison and Kirk (1990), for example, adopting the brilliantly succinct formula, 'Do, Review, Learn, Apply', and using this for the title of their important book, look at the process in a particularly accessible way.

Experiential learning, we might argue, forms the core of what teacher training is 'all about'. Yes, trainees are inducted into a broad policy context for post-compulsory education (what FENTO/LLUK describe as 'the place of FE within the wider world'); they are taught how to draft lesson plans, prepare useful handouts and so on. But at the very heart of their professional learning, and their preparation for a career in teaching, lie the realities of the classroom. Coping with these realities, responding to the challenges they pose, and effectively managing student learning within the constraints presented by them, can all be enhanced by mentors' skills in facilitating experiential learning.

For a trainee, this type of learning will be highly appropriate to what is currently specified by FENTO as 'key area of teaching g':

> Reflecting upon and evaluating one's own performance and planning future practice, [involving] being able to:
> g1 evaluate one's own practice
> g2 plan for future practice
> g3 engage in continuing professional development.
> (FENTO 2000)

If there is one set of constructs which the great majority of mentors will already have encountered it is that concerned with *reflection*. The idea of 'the reflective practitioner' (Schon 1983) permeates virtually all initial teacher training programmes, and has done for some time now, certainly since the early 1990s. This means that many mentors will have encountered it, in one version or another, in their own training. What my intention is now, however, is to look at ways of applying the ideas of reflective practice – and experiential learning as it is so strongly related as a model – to mentoring as a strategy for enhancing professional learning. Given the claims being made for the centrality of experiential learning, what then ought we to understand of its essentials?

A number of names are associated with what is now a very significant body of work examining the links between experience, learning and personal or professional development. The boundaries between the perspectives which these writers have, in turn, presented are sometimes rather blurred ones. It would be unprofessional to contend that any one model simply 'recycles' the contents of an earlier one, though each does have its own distinctive interpretation of the processes involved in reflecting on experience, learning from this and 'moving on'. The significance attached to a cyclical dimension of such a set of actions is far greater in certain models (especially, say, Kolb 1984) than others (notably Schon's formulation). The similarities and overlapping territory are, however, evident.

Interestingly, what it was that originally struck Donald Schon, and which led him to the focus of his seminal work *The Reflective Practitioner: How Professionals Think in Action* was that in his view universities' particular view of knowledge 'fosters selective inattention to practical competence and professional artisanry' (1983: vii). He examines a number of what he called 'vignettes of practice' drawn from fields such as architecture and engineering, concentrating in particular 'on episodes in which a senior practitioner tries to help a junior one learn to do something' (ibid.: viii). It is not that easy, or legitimate, to attempt to encapsulate all of Schon's ideas, which he illustrates by use of his 'vignettes', but it is certainly worth drawing attention to one of his most significant contentions; this is that many professionals, to paraphrase, are at risk of becoming locked into a mode of practice where their technical expertise and rationality is not interrogated. Their knowledge of why they act in certain ways (e.g. when dealing with a client) remains tacit, and they 'find nothing in the world of practice to occasion reflection'. (ibid.: 69). This fact limits both their ability to deal with novel ('surprising' is the word Schon uses) situations and to communicate with others what has been informing their approach to a particular 'case', beyond restating the relevant 'technical' principles.

For practitioners, such as Schon is alluding to here, 'uncertainty is a threat; its admission a sign of weakness' (ibid.). What is proposed in *The Reflective*

Practitioner – one of its key elements – is that professional behaviour will become more insightful, responsive to the novelty of 'cases' *and* susceptible to clear articulation to other professionals if the merits of what the author described as *reflection-in-action* were to be acknowledged and its use to become 'broader, deeper and more rigorous' (ibid.). Reflection-in-action promotes an open enquiry into the *why* of professional acts alongside the simple description of what form these acts have taken. It is true that some practitioners are acknowledged by Schon to already engage in reflection-in-action, but what he argues for is that it should become 'a dominant pattern of practice' (ibid.: 354). In our present context, that of mentoring, the reciprocal benefits which are likely to accrue from this development are ones which are, I hope, quite evident.

An especially accessible version of the central tenets of experiential learning is to be found in Bill Dennison and Roger Kirk's *Do, Review, Learn, Apply* (1990). These authors are primarily concerned with how teachers may create and manage opportunities for experiential learning in learner groups. They are therefore concerned with the teacher–student relationship. However, what is interesting about Dennison and Kirk's framework is that it is so eminently transferable from this context to that of mentoring activities. For example, the authors try to steer teachers away from a didactic, transmissive style and towards one in which their principal strategy becomes *organising opportunities* for learners to move through the cycle of learning begun by *doing* (the 'concrete experience' of Kolb's formulation). They, furthermore, put forward a notion that it is possible to set up successive cycles, from each of which something of significance is learnt. The incremental nature of learning is thus neatly underscored, but more importantly, the confidence-building nature of the process is emphasised: 'Perceptions about success attract students towards more learning cycles . . . there is no more effective means of boosting confidence and raising enthusiasm than the successful completion of a learning cycle' (ibid.: 20–1).

The authors convincingly relate their Do, Review, Learn, Apply (DRLA) model to Kolb's idea of a learning cycle, as shown in Figure 3.1.

I do not believe it is at all tenuous to maintain that what was originally being proposed as a device for enhancing student learning also has much to offer mentors *planning how to structure the professional learning of their trainees*. The DRLA model can be successfully adopted as part of the mentoring repertoire by:

- organising experiences which will represent an appropriate level of challenge (e.g. a particular class to teach; a stipulation that a particular learning resource is incorporated into a session);

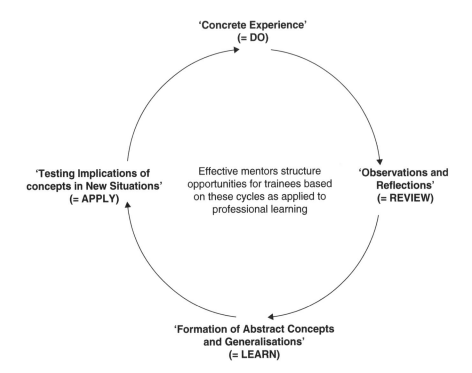

'Concrete Experience'
(= DO)

'Testing Implications of
concepts in New Situations'
(= APPLY)

Effective mentors structure
opportunities for trainees based
on these cycles as applied to
professional learning

'Observations and
Reflections'
(= REVIEW)

'Formation of Abstract Concepts
and Generalisations'
(= LEARN)

Figure 3.1 The relationship between 'DRLA' and Kolb's Learning Cycle

- providing ample opportunities to discuss the professional learning deriving from the experience (especially in the context of post-observation debriefing);

- encouraging trainees to record their reflections on the experience and, especially, to identify ways in which any generalisable principles seem to emerge from the experience (this stage can be worked through using the self-evaluation section of teaching observation proformas which is almost always now provided, and/or in trainees' reflective logs);

- negotiating with trainees how they will implement whatever refinements to their professional practice they now, having been around the cycle, see as being worthwhile.

What is of real value here is the role of the mentor in using DRLA to assist a trainee to move out of their 'comfort zone'. Trainees, in being stimulated to review how things might be better/could be refined, will thus be focusing on what they will do differently; they will not have the safety and comfort of knowing for certain that a change in strategy will achieve better results, but at least they will try such a change rather than simply opting for a repetition of what they have done before.

As noted later on in this guide, reflective practice has not been without its detractors. One criticism that might be worth mentioning at this stage, given the claims I make for being able to link critical reflection with consequential action, is that of Cornford, who believes a

> weakness inherent in many reflective paradigms is the failure to take account of a long recognised problem in human learning – forgetting. Simply being critical is not enough to guarantee that those critical thoughts will be remembered or that those thoughts can be translated into effective procedural action.   (Cornford 2002: 228)

Perhaps the message for mentors embodied in this particular view is that they will need to *revisit* significant matters, over a period of time, in much the same way as we build reviews of student learning into our designs for covering any syllabus with a group. This is to advocate no more nor less than working to a 'spiral syllabus' model, rather than one where topics, once covered, are only encountered again at the summative assessment stage.

'Stages' and mentoring

There is a fundamental connection between the stage of professional development a trainee is at and the nature (or stage) of the mentoring which will be most appropriate. One possibly useful theoretical construct which can be drawn on to illustrate this proposition is that of the 'dichotomies' which Dubin (1961) believed it was possible to identify, and which a number of other writers have subsequently elaborated upon.

Figure 3.2 From unconscious to conscious *incompetence*; from conscious to unconscious *competence* (after Dubin 1961)

A summary version of the dichotomies is shown as Figure 3.2.

What is at the core of Dubin's model are contrasts relating to self-knowledge; no particular claims were made for the applicability of the ideas to the specifics of mentoring, but nevertheless, such an application does seem entirely valid. Some diagrammatic representations of the dichotomies show them ascending a 'staircase', i.e. with UI on the lowest step and UC on the highest; this may in fact be the form in which the model is most accessible to mentors.

In the mentoring context, what we can conceive of is a scenario where, initially, trainees make mistakes (are incompetent) *because they do not appreciate how or why they are such.* This, earliest, stage of their starting to teach is, then, when they are unconsciously incompetent, and – from the mentor's perspective – especially merit a tolerant and patient approach. More importantly, what they also need, to allow them to move to the stage of '*conscious* incompetence', is an opportunity to discuss *why* whatever it is they have done (or have failed to do) is not good practice; the reasons will generally emerge through a skilfully managed discussion, although ultimately mentors may need to recourse to a measure of exposition to allow these to surface.

Once a trainee appreciates the need to refine their practice in a particular regard, the mentor will then suggest (and facilitate if need be) further opportunities for them to experiment. The trainee at this stage will be, more often than not, highly self-conscious (especially if being observed) but – it is hoped – 'getting it right', rather than repeating their earlier mistakes. This stage would accord with Dubin's notion of *conscious competence* – or a state which some observers of teaching have compared with the careful, 'by the book', road skills of many newly licensed drivers; they are (or so it is said) highly aware of all their actions in operating the controls of the car, keeping strictly to speed limits and responding appropriately and courteously to other road users and so on.

The mentor's role at this conscious competence stage would be to comment on any remaining infringements of the best practice guidelines which had been discussed with a trainee. Having already raised the trainee's consciousness concerning particular flawed facets of their classroom practice, they consequently need feel somewhat less hesitant in offering their criticism.

To pursue the analogy with learning to drive, for the teacher, as with the driver, a stage comes in their experience when, to a greater or lesser extent, they perform on the basis of 'second nature'. Obviously, we have now arrived at the *unconscious competence* stage, where we do not have to stop to think about every single classroom action.

It is, though, only appropriate to point out here that a 'dichotomies' framework may have certain serious limitations within the kind of timespan over which we know a teacher-training programme extends – as little as eight or nine months in the case of a full-time, pre-service course. It could well be that there is simply insufficient developmental time available to trainees for them to arrive at the unconscious competence stage, and that this will only be a feature of their later professional development – perhaps of Huberman's 'stabilisation' phase, which he felt dawned only after four to six years of classroom experience (Huberman 1992: 127).

On the other hand, some mentors – and, more broadly, educationalists – may feel that teachers should never become so unself-conscious that they cease from constant self-monitoring. They may become *more conscious of their learner groups than of themselves*, using their 'antennae' to pick up how successfully a lesson is turning out (and modifying its pitch and pace in line with the 'signals' they are receiving), but they never totally lose a measure of self-awareness, and a consciousness of why they are teaching using a certain strategy or mix of strategies.

The Dreyfus model of skills acquisition is an interesting, much-cited one which also hinges on the notion of 'stages', a few aspects of each of which I indicate below, with professional skills developing through the following stages:

- Level 1 – **Novice** (where, for example, there will be a 'rigid adherence to taught rules or plans');
- Level 2 – **Advanced beginner** (here 'situational perception' is still limited);
- Level 3 – **Competent** (an interesting feature of this stage being 'coping with crowdedness');
- Level 4 – **Proficient** (where 'decision-making is less laboured'); and
- Level 5 – **Expert** (by which stage there exists not only an 'intuitive grasp of situations based on tacit understanding' but a 'vision of what is possible').

(Dreyfus and Dreyfus 1986)

Mentors will, in general, be working with individuals progressing through levels 1 to 3, but some trainees may of course display skills development beyond these stages by the end of their programmes – while, out of modesty, some mentors might not claim to have arrived at the 'Expert' stage.

A number of authors have given special prominence to far more explicit notions of actual *mentoring* 'life cycles' or 'stages', seeing these as fundamental to our knowledge of how mentoring works. Healy and Welchert touch on this idea, dealing, for example, with the issue of what may happen at 'the separation juncture' when both parties must 'either redefine their relationship based on collegiality or suffer a deteriorating alliance' (1990:20). This question can be seen to have special resonance in situations where the trainee has also been a colleague training on an in-service basis.

However, fuller treatments of the ideas about the stages which mentoring relationships go through can probably be found in such forays into this area as those of Kram (1983). This is a rather more complex approach than can be readily summarised here, but a most succinct perspective on the concept of 'stages' which is worth mentioning is that promoted by the Centre for Excellence in Leadership (CEL 2004). This simple model sees the mentoring process which best facilitates learning and development as moving through only three stages:

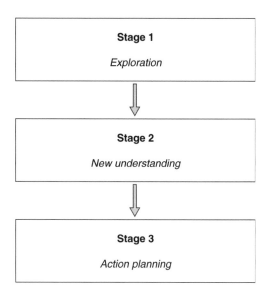

Figure 3.3 One possible interpretation of 'stages' in mentoring (after CEL 2004)

This may appear to oversimplify what is entailed in mentoring processes, discounting, for example, the possibility of the rejection by mentees[1] of ideas which they may have been encouraged to 'explore'. However, it seems to serve quite well as the kind of basic framework which could be presented to trainees as an accessible explanation of 'what mentoring is all about'.

Note

1. In this case, senior college managers who have themselves elected to be mentored.

References

CEL (2004) *Mentoring: Learning from Practice, Learning from Each Other*. London: Centre for Excellence in Leadership.

Cornford, I. R. (2002) 'Reflective teaching: empirical research findings and some implications for teacher education'. *Journal of Vocational Education and Training*, **54**(2), 219–35.

Dennison, B. and Kirk, R. (1990) *Do, Review, Learn, Apply: A Simple Guide to Experiential Learning*. Oxford: Blackwell.

Dreyfus, H. L. and Dreyfus, S. E. (1986) *Mind Over Machine: The Power of Human Intuition and Expertise in the Era of the Computer*. Oxford: Blackwell.

Dubin, R. (1961) *Human Relations in Administration with Readings and Cases*. Englewood Cliffs, NJ: Prentice-Hall.

Eraut, M. (1994) *Developing Professional Knowledge and Competence*. London: Falmer Press.

FENTO (2000) *Standards for Teaching and Supporting Learning in Further Education in England and Wales*. London: Further Education National Training Organisation.

Hargreaves, D. (1999) 'Ask the experts'. *Times Educational Supplement*, 12 February.

Healy, C. C. and Welchert, A. J. (1990) 'Mentoring relations: a definition to advanced research and practice'. *Educational Researcher*, **19**(9), 17–21.

Huberman, M. (1992) 'Teacher development and instructional mastery', in Hargreaves, A. and Fullan, M. G. *Understanding Teacher Development*. New York: Teachers College Press.

Kolb, D. A. (1984) *Experiential Learning. Experience as the Source of Learning and Development*. Englewood Cliffs, NJ: Prentice-Hall.

Kram, K. E. (1983) 'Phases of the mentor relationship'. *Academy of Management Journal*, **26**(4).

Schon, D. (1983) (2nd edn 1991) *The Reflective Practitioner: How Professionals Think in Action*. Aldershot: Arena.

Young, M., Lucas, N., Sharp, G. and Cunningham, B. (1995) *Teacher Training for the FE Sector: Training the Lecturer of the Future*. London: Post-16 Education Centre, Institute of Education, University of London.

Observing classroom teaching

Chapter objectives:

- To outline the rationale for observations.
- To illustrate best practice.
- To provide certain important cautions relating to this activity.

> T4: With Michael Cohen observing. I have never seen those tough nuts being coy before! I wonder if my own nervousness communicated itself to them.
>
> (Otty 1972)

This particular aspect of mentoring in colleges merits a whole chapter to itself for reasons which might appear obvious. In fact, even giving the issue this much prominence does not match the attention it has received with regard to other sectors of education; a fuller treatment of aspects of observation may be found, for example, in Ted Wragg's excellent book *An Introduction to Classroom Observation*, focusing on school teaching (Wragg 1999). Much of the advice this contains is eminently transferable to college contexts.

That they know they will be observed teaching is, almost without exception, the single most important obstacle facing trainees. From long experience as a teacher trainer I would say that the anxieties this aspect of training and assessment engenders are greater than those caused by virtually any other dimension of ITE programmes.

Of course, there are exceptions to this view, and I would not wish to appear dogmatic. Every now and again we encounter trainees who, for example (and as alluded to elsewhere in this guide), have already completed short, but intensive, programmes such as ESOL-focused courses, as offered by CELTA, and where observation has traditionally been 'a part of the grammar' of what takes place each week. Frequently, video or audio recording of peer teaching has even been included. For someone who has already experienced this kind of approach, there will be far less that is novel or intimidating about having a tutor or mentor in the classroom observing how things are going. The presence of the figure at the back of the room with a clipboard is, to a far lesser degree, a worrying matter.

In a slightly different vein, there do always seem to be individuals who are so naturally confident, extroverted or, in some cases, used to 'performing' (former actors, for instance, now undergoing training in the teaching of Drama or Performing Arts) that they are quite unfazed by the prospect of observation. Such trainees are naturally advantaged when it comes to observation, at the very least because they appear able to mask any nervousness they might be experiencing.

From the mentors' perspective, conducting an observation of a trainee is perhaps the best opportunity which will present itself – especially at the debriefing stage – for assisting someone to jump across a gap (or a gulf in some cases) between their present performance and what is desired. Put in extremely simple form, diagrammatically, the presence of a mentor on the right side of such a gap can make the crucial difference between a trainee's practice evolving or fossilising (see Figure 4.1).

Some essential preliminaries

Observation of a trainee's class should never take place in any kind of vacuum. It is essential that a number of issues are addressed, almost literally, before the mentor ever sets foot in the trainee's classroom, and it is such issues with which we are concerned in what follows.

Ideally, a *staged approach* to constructing a trainee's teaching programme will have been adopted, although in the case of employed trainees this will only rarely have been the case. On the route to providing opportunities for

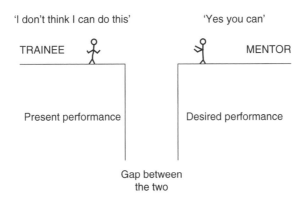

Figure 4.1 Improving trainees' performance by confidence-building

autonomous teaching in their own classrooms, mentors might consider structuring a programme, allowing trainees to progress through some or all of the following stages:

- circulating among learners working independently or in small groups to assist with tasks already set up by a mentor or a 'host' teacher;
- taking responsibility for the work of a segment of the class, perhaps even half of a learner group (which can work especially well in situations where a free room allows for the segment to 'overspill');
- observing a mentor or host teaching the introductory half of a session and then, by prior arrangement, 'picking up' and teaching the rest of the session to its conclusion;
- team teaching, where mentor (or host) alternate their contributions to exposition, handling Q&As or managing task-based work; and
- teaching every second or third lesson, before working continuously with a group.

My rationale in advocating these kinds of interim stages between 'only observing' and autonomous teaching is simply that beginning teaching loses its 'cliff-edge' or 'in at the deep end' feel. Most trainees will embrace such opportunities, only extremely unusually viewing the stages organised by a mentor as evidence of some lack of trust or confidence in their abilities.

Assuming that these kinds of considerations have, so far as possible, been addressed, then the most sensible starting point immediately pre-observation is simply setting out for the person who is going to be observed such things as:

- the *rationale* for observation;
- the *status* of the observation to be conducted;
- the *format* of the observation; and
- the most appropriate '*behaviour*' of the observer.

To deal with each of these in turn:

Rationale for observation

What is meant here is that the mentor lays out the reasons why the trainee is going to be observed, the context for observation in the PCET sector generally and the benefits which, it is hoped, will come about as a result of the exercise.

Mentors might, for example, draw attention to the fact that for any 'licence to practise', practical skills have to be assessed alongside theoretical knowledge: no driver, airline pilot or surgeon can be certificated solely on the basis of their grasp of theory, and it is only fitting that this kind of criterion applies equally to new teachers (who certainly have, it could be argued, almost the same potential to cause harm if their professional expertise has not been appropriately tested).

The requirements of the specific training provider, and the recommendations of the Inspectorate (OfSTED 2003), can be cited as well, of course.

Alongside covering the above points, the routinisation of classroom observation in the sector can usefully be stressed. As in other phases of education, classrooms can no longer be conceived of as 'secret gardens' in which teachers' interaction with learners is in some ways very much a private, individual affair with little or no scrutiny being applied to it. In several contexts, being observed has become commonplace and there are real benefits to be gained from trainees becoming acclimatised to this fact at an early stage. Although, as indicated, many people are nervous or hesitant about being observed, it is virtually always something about which greater confidence and calmness develop the more often observation is experienced. It is worth making clear that right from the point where trainees apply for first (or subsequent) posts, observation will be a feature of their lives. Besides its increasing use as part of selection processes (where, besides ten-minute presentations, actual lessons taught to actual learners are sometimes now required of applicants), observation will be encountered as part of probation, appraisal, peer review structures and the kinds of internal reviews used in institutions to ensure their 'inspection-readiness'. And, of course, the importance of observation within the inspection regime itself can be highlighted.

It is also very worthwhile trying to demonstrate empathy with a trainee by recounting one's own experience of being on the receiving end of observation. Trainees may, on occasion, not connect with the notion that their observers themselves have had to be seen working with groups, and might even have experienced 'nerves'. 'If I did it, so too can you' is the approach being alluded to in Figure 4.1 (p. 67).

Status of observation

Observation takes place for a variety of purposes, and not all of these can be ranked as of equal status. For example, initially mentors may suggest to trainees that they sit in on classes on an entirely *informal* basis – perhaps just to be 'on hand' in case any early practical problems arise with which the trainee might value some support. It is important that mentors make quite clear that if things go wrong for trainees on such occasions then nothing is being 'recorded, and might be used as evidence'. The trainee needs to feel that the observer's presence is motivated wholly by positive reasons to do with support, and the opportunity to provide some initial, friendly feedback on how first 'close encounters' (Cunningham 2000) have looked.

There are differences between observations being conducted for *formative* purposes – in reality, the majority of ITE-related observations will fall into this category – and ones where a *summative* statement of some kind (and possibly a grading for the observed session) will be the end product.

The status of observations can be, to some degree, negotiable: the trainee's readiness for a formal, recorded observation should, wherever possible, be arrived at by taking their own views strongly into account. In situations where a trainee appears especially, but without any real foundation, hesitant regarding formal observation, it may be worth using such strongly encouraging, positive language as 'but you really do seem to me to have settled in, and are confident enough with the group to do well in a formal observation'.

Format of observation

This term covers such matters as informing trainees whether an *observation proforma* will be used, and for what purpose. If so, it is extremely valuable to discuss what is going to be recorded in the respective sections of any such proforma. This gives the trainee a sense of what will be looked for. Mentors can say things like 'This part asks me to comment on whether your aids to learning [boardwork, handouts, video clips and so on] were well integrated into the session.'

It is possible, without being guilty of unethical behaviour, to even illustrate the kinds of comments that have been made on previous trainees. This should bring into pre-observation discussions a helpful sense of the ways in which any comments on flaws in a lesson have been complemented by constructive suggestions for improvements. Clearly, it is important to ensure that the identity of the previous observee is not made known as a result of showing a trainee this sort of material. (The most open mentors may feel comfortable in sharing with a trainee the contents of observation reports they have received on their own practice. As a strategy for deepening the mentoring relationship this has much to commend it, but, of course, it does carry with it a very special risk.)

In connection with the use of observation proformas it is evidently important that a trainee is not kept in the dark about the readership of whatever report is being written. Is it exclusively for the trainee, to inform their own reflections? Is it one to be held only in the mentor's files? Or is it a document which will be read by such figures as a departmental manager, a staff development manager/co-ordinator, someone with a personnel function and/or a representative of the training provider (e.g. most usually a university tutor)?

Also under the heading of the 'format' of the observation we could perhaps consider whether the mentor should be in any significant way a participant in the observed session, but this issue is addressed in connection with aspects of mentor 'behaviour' below.

Observer behaviour

As well as being explicit about whether notes will be taken, a proforma completed, etc., mentors should negotiate such aspects of the observed session as *how it will be presented to learners.* Does the trainee want to say anything to the learner group to explain the presence of the observer? Should the mentor – especially if the group is one which they themselves have taught, or are currently teaching – take on this role? Or should nothing at all be communicated to the group, in the hope that this will minimise any effects ('observer effects') on learners' behaviour? It is, in reality, all but impossible to achieve a state of affairs where a group is entirely unaware of an additional presence in the classroom; so, on balance, it probably is worth saying something by way of explanation, even if this only comprises a neutral statement that X is 'visiting the group today'.

It is only considerate to plan on being as unobtrusive as possible in an observed class; 'back of the room' will usually be best for both trainee and learners – less intimidating for the former, less distracting for the latter. But the question 'And where would you prefer me to sit?' is only courteous and considerate.

However, whatever steps an observer might take to minimise a trainee's stress on being observed, sometimes this emotion may still be all too evident: the true, autobiographical story told in the excellent, multi-award-winning film *An Angel at My Table* (1990), contains the depiction of an extremely harrowing moment in the New Zealand writer Janet Frame's brief career as a primary school teacher. Her polite, understated observer (an inspector, it appears) mostly 'does the right thing' in Janet's classroom, yet she is still reduced to a mute, panic-stricken creature who ends up fleeing (and, sadly, giving up teaching).

The extent to which an observer should participate in a lesson is an interesting question to dwell upon. What needs to be negotiated and agreed is whether the mentor will actually participate, and if so, in what ways. Would the trainee wish their observer to 'make up a pair', for example, if the attendance in a learner group on the date of the observation results in an uneven number? If supported individual work on tasks is in progress, does the trainee feel that they would value some assistance, so that each learner is more likely to be seen? (Or would they, on the other hand, prefer to get a sense, themselves, of what having to cope unaided with the challenge of circulating to all 20 students in a group feels like?) If a trainee 'gets stuck' or forgets a fact – or gets one badly wrong – should the mentor intervene? If technical problems arise with hardware such as a video monitor or OHP, should the mentor try to help? More often than not, the answer in these scenarios will be 'No', and the matter is one to be dealt with at the debriefing stage. However, on occasion, a trainee may well ask for supportive interventions, and make clear that they would not feel undermined by such. It is simply an issue – one of many in teacher education – on which trying to arrive at a hard-and-fast ruling is probably unproductive.

Some mentors find it of value to speak to learners (e.g. while they are working independently on tasks) to try to ascertain whether they have been enjoying a lesson and have properly understood the material being taught. This is an especially sensitive area for trainees, however, and definitely ought only to be engaged in if agreement for it has been reached in advance. A profound sense of insecurity could result from a trainee not knowing why an observer had started talking to learners in their group.

Some further practical considerations

Much of what follows will perhaps seem simply good sense, while some aspects of the advice could seem rather difficult to put into practice. However, each of these practical dimensions of observation and debriefing forms part of what would now be generally considered essentials.

Reaching agreement on what is to be observed

It is especially important, in particular when conducting a *first formal* observation of a trainee's classroom practice, that mutual agreement has been reached as to the group that will be involved. This is an especially vulnerable time for many trainees, and it is crucial that they feel that they will be seen with a group which will allow them to best demonstrate their developing teaching strengths. Wherever possible, therefore, it is advisable to fall in with the trainee's wishes in this regard.

Clearly, over the course of subsequent observations, it would serve neither the trainee's interests nor a mentor's, if only those classes – perhaps those posing fewest teaching challenges – were to be observed. In reality, hardly any class should ever be considered 'off limits' as far as observation is concerned; but exceptions do exist, in the form, for example, of community-based, outreach 'single sex' classes – sometimes provided for women-only groups of language learners, where participation in learning might be otherwise problematic. Teaching such groups is a highly feminised activity in which a male observer's presence would simply run contrary to the spirit of this kind of provision.

In articulating this point of view, mentors might need to draw attention to the fact that being observed with a 'difficult' group need not necessarily be a bad thing, or an event which is inevitably going to drag down the quality of any overall assessment of teaching competence. It does require a particular type of openness to allow an observer into a class where a trainee is experiencing more 'frustration' than 'feel good'; mentors will need to acknowledge this, praise a trainee's agreement that such a class be seen and spell out the potential benefits of their having access to an objective view of where and why problems might be arising. (Interestingly, on a number of occasions I have been asked by trainees quite specifically to come in to see them with classes in which things don't seem to be going at all well; the requests are ones I have always viewed as being only sensible, and evidence of maturity.) Some training programmes actually require mentors to construct teaching timetables for trainees which take account not only of levels, target qualifications etc., but also the range of *motivation* seen across different groups. This may well have points in its favour, although mentors often have a sense of protectiveness which steers them away from putting especially hard-to-motivate groups on a trainee's timetable.

As well as agreeing on the teaching group to be observed, there are such other important considerations involved as the date/notice period that might be appropriate. No trainee, even those with the greatest strengths in their developing skills, reacts well to feeling that an observation has been 'sprung on them'. Wherever possible, a notice period of at least a week is advisable. If trainees say they are happy with less than this, then that, of course, is their decision. (Shorter notice periods may, however, not mesh well with mentors' own schedules and commitments, and it is quite legitimate to point this out.)

A further extremely important factor which needs to be taken into account concerns the importance of observing trainees in a range of settings over a course of training. It is not acceptable, or sound practice, to, say, only observe someone working in a one-to-one setting; e.g. giving individual support in a college's drop-in centre, or circulating to assist individual learners with independent, project-based work. On the other hand, only observing a trainee working in lecture mode cannot provide us with any real insights into the confidence they might display in setting up and managing small-group work (or indeed in giving individual support).

Similarly, mentors ought to beware of the risks attached to consistently observing a trainee working only with learners at a very restricted range of qualification levels (or, worst of all, only at one level). A PGCE or a CertEd is – at the risk of restating the obvious – a *licence to practise*, and as such can really only legitimately be awarded where competence has been demonstrated in a range of settings. *Equipping Our Teachers for the Future* certainly points to the need for trainees 'to gain a good understanding of the range of learners in this diverse sector' (DfES 2004a: 11). The ability of trainees to work effectively across such a range (insofar as it is possible within any one institution) should be monitored by mentors.

Mentors also need to acknowledge that in any one observation there are only so many aspects of classroom competence which can be demonstrated. Textbooks on effective teaching, the nature of the inspection framework and much of the advice provided by trainers all give emphasis to the issue of *variety*, and accommodating a range of learner preferences within lessons is sometimes seen as the 'holy grail' of good teaching.

In some respects, rather than being positively challenged by all this, trainees can experience a real anxiety that in a particular observed session there will be insufficient evidence for their ability to adopt varied, inclusive approaches; one hears trainees apologise for there being 'no groupwork in the lesson today', 'no handout to go with what's being covered' or 'no transparencies'. What is important is to offer reassurance that it is fully accepted that in, say, a session lasting only 60 or 90 minutes, the range of strategies which can be deployed will not be comprehensive. There will be instances in certain specialisms where the whole of a session may need to be devoted to a single activity. It may be quite legitimate, and necessary, for a Performing Arts teacher to sometimes, for example, have her group engaged in intense rehearsal for a forthcoming production. Similarly, in the Art and Design studio a learner group may need to spend the whole of a session continuing to work on a project brief, and the trainee's role will entirely consist of circulating, monitoring learners' performance and offering individual guidance.

It is important, of course, to promote variety (perhaps based on the idea of most learners' attention spans, according to one theorist at least, being only 20 minutes or so (Buzan 1982). However, the more important objective to negotiate with trainees should be that of building in variety over a *series* of lessons, so that a group always has the anticipation of different stimuli being on their classroom menu. Attention to the need for such variety can be encouraged by pointing to the way in which a proper, appropriately detailed scheme of work for a group should include a log of which activities/aids to learning are planned on a week-by-week basis. A separate 'Variety Planner', in grid format, is a very worthwhile alternative and has the added advantage of giving both trainee and mentor an immediate visual impression of the ways in which one session has differed from another. Resembling a register, with dates at the top of each column of the grid, the planner then simply shows which methods/materials were 'present' for each session – and which were 'absent'.

The observation itself

The importance of positioning and clarifying the degree of participation (if any) which the observer may have has already been described. Equally important are considerations to do with body language and gesture. Some observers may find it extremely difficult to avoid communicating *non-verbally* that, from their perspective, a lesson is not going as well as they would like. Yet if we are not able to understand an instruction a trainee has given to a group, or cannot see the point of an activity which is being set up, it is all too easy to show our confusion and perplexity. It calls for a surprisingly high degree of self-awareness to know that we are looking puzzled, disappointed or generally unhappy with the classroom proceedings we are witnessing. Yet it is really very important that we make strong efforts in this regard, so that the confidence of the person being observed is not undermined. We will probably all, at some stage or another, observe lessons which leave us shaking our head, but we must attempt to limit this to a mental process before it becomes a visible, physical one.

A further challenge lies in balancing the demands of the documentation attached to an observation with actually watching what is going on in the lesson. Occasionally I have heard trainees express real doubts that an observer can possibly have properly *seen* a lesson in action, because they have spent so much of their time with their head down, completing an observation proforma. It is true that this kind of criticism has most usually correlated with training schemes that have adopted particularly cumbersome, multi-page observation documents.

Where the paperwork is indeed complex, rather than concise (and the variations seen are many), then there are arguments for simply making handwritten notes which will form the basis of the debriefing, and completing the required forms at a later stage. If this tactic is adopted, however, trainees do need reassuring that the content of any formal report will accurately reflect what was noted and communicated in the debriefing. Mentors who are fortunate in being able to write speedily and legibly will be able to compile formal reports while observing (perhaps tidying up/concluding them while trainees are sending off their groups, gathering up their lesson materials and so on). Some training providers encourage mentors to complete electronic versions of observation (and other) reports, and this facility is particularly worth exploiting where one's handwriting is not always that clear or where it is simply a mentor's preference to work in this way rather than using 'snail mail' to submit reports.

There is a real skill in being able to juggle between the need to watch a lesson, especially how learners are responding to it (and from the back of the room it will not be at all easy to see facial expressions, for example), and remaining mindful of what the observation documentation requires of mentors. The situation might be said to be somewhat comparable to taking photographs of events or landscapes, when a concern with correct use of the camera (or, in certain 'tourist' contexts, perhaps feeling uncomfortable about using photography at all to 'capture' people and places) can be such a preoccupation that the subject itself is at risk of becoming of secondary importance.

Use of timings

It can be useful to add to observation comments being made occasional in-text or margin notes (much as on a lesson plan) indicating times. In a general sense these can serve to provide additional evidence that mentors were watching classroom proceedings closely. Moreover, they can be helpful in allowing a trainee to see where a lesson segment which was ostensibly introductory ran on for an unnecessarily long time, or where a concluding segment, including a recapitulation, was squeezed into far too little of the lesson as a whole. Any serious misalignments with the proposed timings will also be evident. Also, if a mentor chooses to total up the respective time allocations to teacher talk, student activity etc., then the proportions of and balance between these will similarly stand out.

Use of quotations

Where possible, it is sometimes valuable to note key phrases from an observed session, whether used by the trainee or a member of a learner group. Mentors can more easily make any necessary debriefing points about, for example, ambiguity of instructions, if they have noted down what exactly was said by the trainee, and the kind of reactions manifested by learners ('I'm sorry, can you say all that again please . . . did you mean . . .?'). This type of component of an observation report/debriefing is of special value in enhancing trainees' learning about their questioning skills, and about the way in which they provide responses to learners' questions. We cannot provide a precise, detailed account of the classroom interaction in the way that it is possible for language-focused research to do (e.g. a 'Barnes-type' analysis, as described in the classic *Language, the Learner and the School* (Barnes *et al.* 1969). What we *can* do, however, is illustrate such interaction at what seems to be key points – of understanding or *mis*understanding – in the session.

Other points to observe

Having been supplied in advance with the *objectives* for a session (and, ideally, having had the chance to discuss these with a trainee), the mentor is able to focus on monitoring progress being made towards meeting these. Were the objectives – perhaps in a paraphrased form – shared with learners? Did the trainee explicitly relate content to these? If segments of what is being taught do not appear to relate well to specified objectives it is problematic, and learners themselves will quite frequently ask why they are on the agenda.

A current favourite of selection panels, who have asked that an applicant describes or actually teaches a short lesson, is the question 'And how exactly would you know that your objectives had been met?' This fact legitimates a mentoring focusing on the *learning checks* which appear to be being used in a session. Are the checks valid; do they cover all the learners in a group? They will not, of course, if only very few group members are targeted in questioning and if oral checks such as this are not supplemented by, say, written work. How many learners in a group were questioned? How many were never asked to provide answers? How were flawed responses managed?

There are also broader, rather more impressionistic and difficult to 'quantify' aspects of a trainee's performance which mentors will need to observe. Is the learning 'climate' conducive to participation, or do the members of a group appear to be uncomfortable? Does the trainee seem 'at home' in the classroom environment, or, at its most extreme, is his/her apparent nervousness actually distracting? Does he/she have any mannerisms of speech or gesture that may represent distractions? Perhaps most importantly, does he/she seem to have connected with what is going on in a room – or possess the 'withit-ness' which a number of observers of teaching feel is crucial in differentiating between effective and ineffective teachers? (This is not always that hard to cite evidence for – we have probably all observed at least one class in which the trainee was unaware of someone reading a magazine or a message on a mobile phone.)

The current FENTO/LLUK (2000) statement (under 'Personal attributes') relating to 'personal impact and presence' is possibly an especially jarring one for some experienced practitioners, but so long as it is included in the organisation's listing of what is important we should bear in mind the need to observe the specifics of how exactly a trainee has made their presence felt within a group – beginning with their strategies for obtaining a quiet start and signalling the focus and value of the observed session. Personally, I would always opt out of using the exact phrasing used by FENTO/LLUK where I needed to feed back to a trainee who appeared to lack the qualities in question. It would be a statement guaranteed to demotivate in my view.

What mentors *can* draw attention to, to add some objectivity to any comments on 'impact and presence', is whether, for instance, a trainee has used the classroom space well – have they circulated around the room, signalling to learners that they will be able to note any off-task behaviour? Have they made eye contact well with a group or have they, on the other hand, talked to the board a lot? How well have they projected their voice?

The debriefing

It is after the observation, at the debriefing stage, that the contribution mentors can make to the professional learning of trainees is, arguably, most significant.

For this reason it is essential to review a number of key dimensions of the activity, which in some regards calls for especially high levels of skill, self-awareness and sensitivity on the part of mentors. A poorly handled debriefing can even lead to withdrawal from a training programme (this is not an exaggeration, but can be readily documented). On the other hand, a successful one – including one taking place after a quite flawed teaching session – can have profoundly positive effects on a trainee's self-esteem and their developing professional practice.

Some starting points

- Having thanked a trainee for agreeing to the observation, wherever possible the aim should be to try to find at least one thing to say about the lesson, in advance of the debriefing, which sends a positive message – that it was enjoyable or that it, or at the very least that the material covered, was interesting. An acknowledgement that accommodating an observer in a classroom can add to the natural stress of teaching is also worthwhile.

- If not previously arranged, a time/date should be set as soon as possible for a meeting to discuss the session (unless it is possible to talk immediately after the session).

- Privacy is essential, so a venue needs to be available where others will not be able to listen to the conversation.

- So, too, is freedom from interruptions, insofar as this state can ever be achieved in busy institutions. A room without a phone, or one in which the phone can be switched off (including, of course, mobile phones) is ideal.

- It is useful to outline what kinds of issues should be covered in the debriefing, including the trainee's own perceptions of a session's strengths and weaknesses.

- The maximum length of the debriefing should be specified.

- A seating arrangement should be striven for in which mentor and trainee can make eye contact, while at the same time both look at any relevant notes, diagrams or materials. From the diagrams below (Figure 4.2) it will be clear that what usually works best is a situation where the centre point is the corner of a table (arrangement 3). (The table can be dispensed with, but it becomes much harder to spread out useful items to which reference is being made.) Sitting opposite each other (arrangement 1) can promote a 'superior/inferior' relationship, while sitting side-by-side (arrangement 2) renders eye contact problematic.

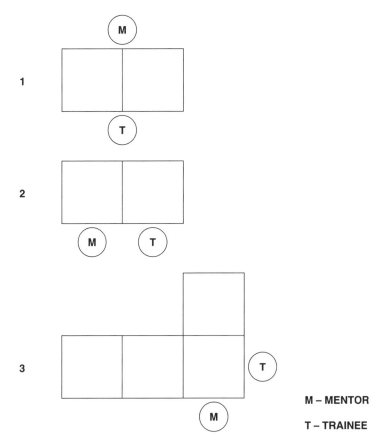

Figure 4.2 Possible seating arrangements for debriefings

Key components of a successful debriefing

'He was so critical, he never mentioned *anything* which had gone well.' This, sadly, quite frequently repeated statement is a useful preface to looking at the substance of the interaction within the debriefing itself. Trainees do seem to be somewhat prone to dwelling on negative points made in the context of debriefing, and it is therefore worth highlighting the value of finding ways in which strengths can be praised. There may have been very few such strengths – in fact, overall, an observed lesson might have been very weak, even one where OfSTED might describe any learning that has taken place to have been despite, rather than as a result of, the teacher's presence, and, by its published criteria, might have been proposing a grade 7 (OfSTED/ALI 2001).

The challenge here is to make necessary criticisms, even very strong ones, as palatable as they can be. We cannot be dishonest and say that a lesson was a success when it clearly was not; this would be unprofessional, would jeopardise our own credibility as practitioners and would serve neither the interests of the trainee or the learners. But the kind of, albeit fairly minimalist, positive statements which can be made to prepare the ground for such strong criticism could include:

'It was good to see a punctual start to the session.'

'You seem to have spent quite a lot of time preparing your materials for today.'

'Your boardwork is nice and neat.'

'I could hear you well at the back of the room.'

'Being observed didn't seem to bother you too much.'

'It seems you know your material.'

'Thanks for letting me have such a neat, clear plan.'

There is, of course, no magical solution to be offered if any of the above statements do not apply. In 'worst possible cases', mentors might only have recourse to something along the lines of: 'Well, we've got quite a lot of issues to talk about today, but I hope to be able to make some positive suggestions about each of these.'

In a number of ways, it is possible to summarise the essential 'criticism' elements in debriefings in tabular form. This allows us to note the critical differences between what is usually referred to as *destructive* criticism and *constructive* criticism (see Table 4.1).

Successful debriefings, as well as simply aiming to incorporate the positive elements shown on the right side of the table, also seem to accord with the following template:

- There is ample space for the trainee's voice to be heard. The useful notion of 'discursive space' allows for a two-way process (the contrast would be with a lecture-format event where, for example, the observer spends the great majority of the debriefing time talking about how they would have taught/would normally teach the session).

- Proceedings include as many questions as possible, ones which encourage trainees to think of alternative strategies and approaches (not single solutions).

- They are based on prioritising issues; not all the flaws in a session will be of equal significance, and the most minor can be overlooked if to include every single failing would produce an overwhelming list of points for attention.

- Language use is sensitive and culturally aware, but is not so vague as to make meaning disappear. Many, if not most, of us aim to be diplomatic and

Table 4.1 *Contrasting destructive and constructive criticisms of classroom practice*

DESTRUCTIVE CRITICISM	CONSTRUCTIVE CRITICISM
● Tone negative/pessimistic	● Tone optimistic/encouraging
● 'Deficits' drawn attention to (What was *not* present/covered)	● 'Credits' highlighted (What *was* accomplished; the strengths of the lesson)
● Largely 'looking back' (as in feed*back*)	● Looking backwards *and* forwards (as in 'feedforward')
● *What* went wrong – all description and no analysis	● Important diagnostic elements – *why* might things be going wrong
● Emphasis on observer's *own* preferred teaching strategies	● Emphasis given to allowing trainee to articulate reasons for *their* preferences
● Extremely few suggestions made regarding improvements	● A range of 'method' suggestions made, and practical illustrations given in these
● No advice on getting support to make improvements	● Offer of targeted support is prominent in the exchange
● Lesson's every flaw reviewed	● Focus on highlighting why some flaws especially worth correcting
● 'Demolition job' on trainee's self-esteem	● Self-esteem enhancement a priority

not blunt about failings we perceive in others' performance. A self-check on whether this has only resulted, however, in vagueness is to ask a trainee if a point is clear, or whether it would be useful to rephrase it.

- The focus is on performance and not personality – the classic advice in this regard is to concentrate on using phrases such as 'And then *what happened was . . .*', rather than 'And then *what you did* was . . .' Note, though, that this is an especially elusive aspect of conducting effective debriefings. Where it seems virtually impossible to avoid reference to an individual trainee's approach to an element of classroom practice which has seemed ill-judged or poorly handled, it can sometimes be married to a confession on the mentor's part that they themselves are occasionally still guilty of whatever it is the mentee has done or failed to do.

- The debriefing's conclusion has two principal parts: a reiteration of any strengths evident in the observed session and agreement regarding the priorities or targets for subsequent observations, signalled by such language as 'So what, overall, would you say were the things we should most concentrate on improving before next time?' It is, furthermore, only good practice for trainees to be invited to follow up any issues on which they have reflected as a result of the debriefing and/or to get in touch where a specific point does not seem either clear or valid. This is, after all, only the kind of reassurance we would wish to offer our learner groups (as indicated by one of the statements in the following framework).

The 'learner perspective'

One alternative, really quite succinct, framework for providing an overview of an observed lesson is based on a simple set of questions regarding the ways in which a lesson was probably *experienced by learners*:

- What was it likely to have felt like being a student in this lesson?
- Could students see the point of the lesson?
- Did they know what to do, and why they were doing it?
- Were they able to get on with their tasks in a well-ordered learning environment, or might some learners have been disrupted?
- Could they see where the lesson fitted into an overall scheme?
- Might they have been baffled by any unexplained new terms/ideas?
- Did they know if/when their understanding of the lesson's content would be assessed (formally or informally)?
- Would they be likely to value, and actually *use*, any 'takeaways' – handouts, notes from OHTs etc.?
- Were they given any pointers as to how to follow up the lesson independently?
- Were less confident learners reassured that there would be a chance to revisit the content if it had been found challenging?
- Did they seem to enjoy it?

One clear advantage which this approach carries with it is that it accords well with the emphasis being placed by the inspectorate and colleges themselves on 'placing the learner at the heart' of what is being done in post-compulsory education. However, it is presented here merely as a basis for thinking about how to debrief a trainee, and cannot encompass all the *details* which will need to come into the mentor–trainee exchange.

Debriefing is perhaps one of those dimensions of the mentoring role where the *artistry* of teaching comes into play. We can conceive of a 'formula' or a 'template', such as those described above, which will allow us to structure the event. But from certain perspectives the risk we run is of a mechanistic approach, where the ability of experienced, competent practitioners to operate on the basis of an informed intuition – their autonomous professional judgement, one might say – is discounted, or at any rate marginalised. Effective debriefing can only be formulaic, i.e. based on science, up to a point. It entails knowledge not only of teaching a subject but also of oneself, a real facility with sensitive oral communication and an ability to listen to and empathise with an individual who may be experiencing some stress. In these ways mentors who have had any exposure at all to certain principles used in counselling are probably advantaged in undertaking their responsibilities, but insofar as 'crafting' a successful debriefing is concerned, the motivation to do so is, finally, what may be most important. It is in this *creative* sense that I have invoked above the idea of 'artistry'.

Some cautions

If we accept just how crucially important observation and debriefing are in the mentoring process, certain cautions may be worth providing.

The use of e-mail in providing feedback

It would be blinkered to fail to recognise the ways in which electronic communications have, in certain ways, been conducive to convenience and saving time and expense. In its important statement on 'equipping our teachers for the future', the Department for Education and Skills points to 'e-mentoring' as having a role to play in the mix of functions performed by mentors (DfES 2004: 15). Yet many people do experience disquiet over some of the more negative consequences of the use of this medium. The neglect of basic courtesies and the use sometimes of really quite abrasive language, which would have been less likely to be encountered, it is claimed, in 'snail mail' or in conversations – at any rate between professionals: have been highlighted. Using e-mail to provide feedback on an observed lesson may, therefore, carry certain risks. Mentors should beware of a harsher tone creeping in, with points being made hurriedly and with less care to construct the sort of tactful, 'kinder' phrasing which face-to-face communication might entail.

Neglect of the liaison function

Although in this section the need for privacy has been noted (in the context of a venue for debriefings) this should not imply that information relating to classroom practice cannot be appropriately shared. Liaison with training institutions is essential in fact. Where a college-based mentor is able to identify targets for a trainee, monitoring of progress in working towards these will be most efficient where any other individual (usually an HE-based tutor) involved in the trainee's programme is apprised of these. (The process should obviously work in the opposite direction, too.) Mentors have a responsibility to share the outcomes of observations with certain other key figures – always taking pains to first communicate to the trainee that this will be taking place, and the reasons for the contact being a valuable part of the training programme.

Over-long lists of 'areas for improvement'

These can be counter-productive; where a trainee's practice has caused concern in a number of regards, there must, subsequently, take place an intelligent selection and ordering of points needing attention. One criterion useful in the construction of such a list is simply how urgent something is. Ought it to be remedied before the very next meeting with a learner group? (Some examples might be extreme inaudibility, illegible boardwork, late arrival of a trainee with no apology provided to a group. These are all aspects of practice which might have immediate negative consequences including causing learners to withdraw from their course.) Are there some less serious concerns which can either be listed separately or saved up? A listing of, say, a dozen problems can seem an insurmountable obstacle to a trainee and they may be demotivated enough by the experience of being given such a list that they might abandon the idea of a teaching career altogether.

Unrealistic expectations

These may unconsciously penetrate mentors' feedback. Avoiding this syndrome calls for a high level of self-awareness, in particular being able to recall being challenged by classroom situations oneself while a practitioner with only limited experience. Among the terminology used by a number of training providers, that of 'beginning teacher' is actually quite helpful as it signifies that a trainee's professional journey is only just beginning. Mistakes that might appear stupid to a teacher with ten years' classroom experience are eminently forgivable ones in someone who has only taught for a total of six hours. In this context, referring to the parallel of craft *apprenticeships* might be helpful, especially as it is arguably true that a trainee is, in reality, the 'apprentice' to the mentor – the 'master' of their craft, to pursue the analogy using the most traditional terminology.

Initial teacher education in the UK is incredibly short when compared to the kind of preparation for a craft which, at least in the past, entailed up to five years' apprenticeship – the length of time which my own father, for one, spent in becoming a carpenter and joiner. Trainees on pre-service courses are in training, typically, for a mere eight months (and on some universities' programmes will not teach at all for the first three months of this, i.e. the autumn term). Even towards the end of this kind of period it is neither realistic nor legitimate to expect the kind of confidence and polish which a 'time-served' craftsman might be expected to display. We can, in other words, expect to see a developing *competency*, but it is highly unlikely that we will witness *mastery*.

To some extent, another perspective which seems to offer mentors a valuable starting point when contemplating how to approach observations and debriefings is that of 'value added'. The arguments in favour of including such a measure in arriving at judgements of school and college learners' attainments, alongside their raw scores in tests and exams, will be well remembered by experienced practitioners. While we cannot adopt the kinds of statistical methods used to demonstrate that learners' achievements – their 'distance travelled' – were frequently more impressive than their results would lead commentators to believe, we can certainly think in terms of trainees' 'baselines'. Individual trainees will all start from different points, e.g. in terms of level of confidence, intuitive grasp of what learners will best respond to, the depth and breadth of their subject knowledge, and so on. If we acknowledge the importance of such baselines it allows for a reorientation of feedback towards an emphasis on progress made.

The issue of grading

Part of the process of *socialising* trainees into the nature of PCET realities is introducing them to the nature of the grading system currently used by OfSTED/ALI in the assessment and inspection of practical teaching. If it is at all helpful to remind mentors of the range of grades, they are as follows:

Grade 1: Outstanding

Grade 2: Very good

Grade 3: Good

Grade 4: Satisfactory

Grade 5: Unsatisfactory

Grade 6: Poor

Grade 7: Very poor

Some pre- and in-service training programmes now require that, in connection with at least one observation conducted by a mentor, a grade is awarded. For some mentors, this will be a possibly contentious, perhaps onerous aspect of their role – and the legitimacy of applying Common Inspection Framework criteria to *beginning* teachers in particular may be questionable. Nevertheless, if grading is to be undertaken it is advisable to stress that:

(a) in most respects mentors' *evaluative comments*, not a grade, will best inform the trainee's reflections and strategies for improvement;

(b) a grade does not equate in any way to a static, immutable state of affairs but only to performance on one day, with a particular learner group; and

(c) from an analysis of grades awarded over time (i.e. since the introduction of the current inspection arrangements in 2001), very few 'top' grades (grade 1s) have been recorded.

Mentors should be aware that trainees being awarded grades such as '3' – which, from most perspectives, would be a perfectly respectable outcome in the context of traineeship – can sometimes feel aggrieved; it is almost as if this particular grade is subconsciously being compared to an honours degree class, i.e. 'a third'.

Hostile reactions to feedback

Most mentors will from time to time have to contend with trainees whose reaction to being given feedback, however skilfully this is done, is hostile, possibly even confrontational. There is a range of possible explanations for this state of affairs. One might simply be that a mentor is considerably younger than the person they are mentoring; many new entrants to PCET teaching, especially those from vocational backgrounds, are fairly mature – perhaps in their 40s or 50s. Receiving criticism from a relatively youthful mentor can sometimes be hard to accept. It is also sometimes said that gender can be a factor in negative situations which develop between mentor and trainee; most usually the situation being described involves a mature male being mentored by a younger female.

We are in the realms of conjecture here. What is probably easier to recognise is the simple fact that when we are commenting on someone's teaching he or she can experience this as reflecting on their identity as human beings. This is why the need to emphasise aspects of *practice*, avoiding, wherever possible, *personalising* criticism, is so important. So, too, is adequately setting the scene for observation/debriefing, and making quite clear to trainees that the process is intended to be, above all, a supportive one, aimed at improving the experience of both trainees and their learners.

If constructively critical comments need to be made (which many observers of teaching would say is virtually inevitable at some stage) then *evidencing* these is also crucial. It is here that the FENTO/LLUK Standards can possess a particular value to mentors in allowing direct references to areas of classroom practice which have *not* been adequately demonstrated. Other ways in which criticism can be substantiated include, for example, the use of the timings/ quotes as advocated previously.

It is worth illustrating for trainees the kinds of 'Yes, but . . .' responses which might be given to feedback, which are so unproductive. A trainee saying what 'normally'/'would have'/'could have' features/featured in a lesson had events of some kind or another not conspired against them is, more often than not, a form of self-defence. Mentors need to ensure, therefore, that they stress that they are not in the business of 'attack'.

I am not advocating aiming for a quiet life by manipulating trainees in such a way that they never interrogate a mentor's criticism and simply agree with everything being said to them. This will not be developmental in any way, as the trainee's responses will be purely 'strategic' ones, i.e. they will be made to 'get the mentor off their back' and to appear co-operative. What we must seek are 'learning' responses, ones which are based on a genuine acceptance of points and guidance being provided by mentors.

All of the above hinges on the effective provision by the mentor of a rationale for observation and debriefing, and appropriate guidance (ground rules) regarding ways in which feedback should be most positively both given and responded to. Stressful exchanges may still arise, and perhaps even cause a mentor to seek support from his or her peers in dealing with these. But there are certainly some steps that individual mentors can take to mitigate the likelihood of conflict with a trainee arising.

Failing to see trainees as individuals

Like every other teacher, you and I are individuals with personalities of our own and teaching approaches which are special to us. Certainly no-one can take over another teacher's ways lock, stock and barrel, apply them, and hope for success.

(Marland 1975: 3)

Although Michael Marland's long-standard work for new teachers on survival in classrooms does go on to remind readers of the existence of a body of transferable principles and techniques, he is right, it seems, in underscoring the individuality which teaching, perhaps above all professions, allows for. He is, to use a phrasing with a greater degree of modernity, warning of the dangers of attempting to clone new teachers in our own likeness.

When describing the kind of mentoring they hope to receive, many trainees express sentiments closely according with these:

'What I hope for from my mentor: support, encouragement, genuine concern for my development. I hope that my mentor will be able to strike the right balance between guiding my learning and allowing me to develop my own ideas and my own teaching style.'   (Trainee on full-time pre-service course, 2004)

Here we can see that, already at the very earliest stages – the quotation was obtained during the first weeks of a trainee's programme – there is a duality of needing pointers but not prescription. The word 'balance' seems of special importance, as used by this trainee. They appear fully accepting of a mentor's role in imparting the benefits of their own experience, and acknowledge the credibility of the mentor to offer guidance. But they are also already finding their own voice, and in an important sense asking that this be heard.

The message for mentors in this far from untypical statement need not be laboured – it is simply that (perhaps especially in the context of giving feedback, as referred to in the preceding section) we should be self-aware enough to judge whether our views are being overly influenced by our own pedagogic preferences. Are we really looking at 'mistakes' – of style or substance – or is it sometimes merely a case of 'Well, it's not really me'? Are approaches which are different from our own always inferior? If something novel is working, perhaps surprisingly, does this threaten us in some way?

As observed elsewhere in this guide, mentors should neither be aiming at standardising professional practice nor presenting single-strategy solutions to problems in learning and teaching. An absolutely fundamental dimension of effective mentoring relationships exists in the plane of generating discursive knowledge about *alternatives*. Clearly we have the responsibility to exercise our professional judgement – and authority – where it is evident that harm may be being done to learners by a trainee's approach. But if advice being given is based solely on the desire to reproduce ourselves as teachers (and possibly also to reproduce our own 'best' teachers – often those who inspired us, earlier on, to enter the profession) then we will struggle to justify this position.

The list of cautions provided here is certainly not intended to be comprehensive. As with virtually all of the components of mentoring, a high degree of learning on the job will come into play with regard to what works well/less well in the observation and discussion of trainees' classroom practice; so, too, will the collaboration and sharing of experience with other mentors which is being strongly advocated at various points in this guide.

References

Barnes, D., Britton, J. and Rosen, R. (1969) *Language, the Learner and the School*. Harmondsworth: Penguin.

Buzan, T. (1982) *Use Your Head*. London: Ariel.

Cunningham, B. (2000) 'Beginning "close encounters": on starting to teach in colleges'. *Teacher Development*, 4(3), 241–56.

DfES (2004) *Equipping Our Teachers for the Future: Reforming Initial Teacher Training for the Learning and Skills Sector*. Nottingham: Department for Education and Skills.

FENTO (2000) Standards for Teaching and Supporting Learning in Further Education in England and Wales. London: Further Education National Training Organisation.

Marland, M. (1975) *The Craft of the Classroom*. London: Heinemann Educational Books.

OfSTED (2003) *The Initial Training of Further Education Teachers: A Survey*. London: Office for Standards in Education [HMI 1762].

OfSTED/ALI (2001) *The Common Inspection Framework*. London: Office for Standards in Education/Adult Learning Inspectorate.

Otty, N. (1972) *Learner Teacher*. Harmondsworth: Penguin.

Wragg, E. C. (1999) *An Introduction to Classroom Observation* (2nd edn). London: Routledge.

5

The challenges and rewards of mentoring

Chapter objective:

- To indicate the range of professional rewards and challenges that mentors will encounter.

'Overall, my mentor has been a great support. I will always appreciate his advice, and will take all I have learnt to my new jobs'.

(Trainee teacher qualifying from a full-time, pre-service course, July 2004)

The rewards

I would like to begin this chapter by paraphrasing a very well known advertising slogan used to attract new entrants to school teaching and say that, quite simply, 'Everyone remembers a good mentor'. Clearly, the view of the trainee quoted above would underscore this claim, and it is a highly affirming way of perceiving the value of this part of a teacher's professional work.

Mentoring is an activity that has almost unparalleled potential to shape the developing skills, and attitudes, of teachers in training. The support given to someone in the early stages of his/her teaching career will be remembered and valued, very probably for the rest of his/her professional life. This fact is, in itself, satisfying, and so often in my experience is evidenced by the ways in which new teachers frequently stay in touch with those who have mentored them.

Clearly, however, mentors would want to have some further positive reasons for committing themselves to the role, given that it is a time-consuming additional duty. It has perhaps been squeezed in alongside a teaching timetable comprising, say, 25 hours' weekly classroom contact and all the other functions now expected of established college teachers.

The nature of the trainee cohort

One dimension of the activity that we can, with some confidence, draw attention to is that, in the main, the new entrants to college teaching are able, committed and well qualified; they are, therefore, individuals for whom a positive professional relationship is a strong likelihood. They are those who should be properly inducted and socialised with because they have a great deal to offer. Helping with adjusting to the realities of post-compulsory education, so that trainees may begin as soon as possible to begin to make valuable contributions, is in itself fulfilling.

Some trainees may have held preconceptions about the nature of the sector (although this is very unlikely if they themselves were college students, e.g. on access courses) and these kinds of issues can act as barriers to their integration into the community of practice they aspire to join. Of course, some of the 'realities' might be quite hard to present in a positive vein, and sometimes it can be difficult to safeguard against contaminating early impressions of the sector with negativity – I am thinking here about such issues as the current lack of parity with school teachers in terms of salary, for instance, or the intrusive form which management strictures regarding student retention can assume. The sheer volume of paperwork which burdens not just college teachers but those working in every area of education is hard to be positive about.

However, it is perhaps useful to note that in McKelvey and Andrews' (1998) study of the perceptions and motivations of trainees, many of the individuals surveyed viewed the acknowledged challenges faced by college teachers as positive ones, and had actually been attracted to the idea of making their mark in a challenging profession. This particular study, furthermore, found that where trainees 'had been well supported by their personal mentors [this] had strengthened their commitment to teaching in FE' (ibid.: 362).

For new entrants with a more limited degree of awareness of what the concerns, norms and preoccupations of the sector are, and on witnessing the sometimes frenetic, and occasionally beleaguered, lives of full-time teachers, there will probably be a sense of disorientation during their first period of contact with real college students. Assisting in shortening any time during which such trainees experience feeling disorientated is a hugely important and satisfying function for mentors to perform. The kind of 'jargon busting' advocated in Chapter 2 can play an important part in this, along with attending to all the small 'housekeeping' matters. Where these are dealt with early on, the phrase 'at home' will more often than not be just the right one to describe how a trainee will rapidly come to feel.

I believe we can also draw attention to such positive reasons for committing to mentoring as those which follow, some of which are further developed in the concluding section of this guide pointing to the links between mentoring and continuing professional development:

Mentoring, professionalism and professional identity

- Recognition by a college of one's own professionalism, both in terms of classroom skills and the ability to maintain effective relations with colleagues. There is a certain status attached to mentoring, and a clear source of professional pride. At West Kent College mentors are described (in the college's *Mentoring Policy*) as being

  - 'regarded by his or her peers with credibility and respect [and]
  - regarded by his or her line manager as a good role model' (WKC 2004).

- The benefits deriving from being stimulated to make plain to a trainee the *why* as well as the *what* of a particular approach to teaching. All mentors are involved in representing and explaining their own practice, and in doing so are caused to move well beyond 'I've always done it this way.' They are steered into analysing the 'it', and interrogating their usual strategies for getting students to discern something interesting, and conceptually manageable, in 'it'. Mentors, to put it slightly differently, stand to *learn* more about why certain approaches work well, and why others might not, in the very act of having to *teach* the underlying principles to their trainees.

- There are satisfactions to be gained from assisting in practical and less practical ways new entrants to teaching to survive what is a demanding environment. Huberman, in writing about how teachers 'survive' their early experiences, describes how 'on the other side of the ledger, the *discovery* theme [includes] having one's own pupils, one's own classroom, materials . . . and of feeling oneself a colleague among peers' (Huberman 1992: 122). It is by facilitating what Huberman refers to as discovery that mentors can bring about for trainees a situation, a state of emotional wellbeing almost, that allows them to tolerate what he depicts as 'survival'. At the core of Huberman's formulation of what it means to discover the positives of professional life as a teacher is quite simply 'feeling at home' – included in the life of an institution – a positive outcome which no one is better placed to bring about than mentors.

- Experienced mentors often happily acknowledge the ways in which their own repertoire of teaching skills and ideas has been extended by contact with a trainee. (Similarly, university tutors will readily talk about the good new ideas being tried out in the classrooms which they are observing, and which they themselves will experiment with in future.)

Jackson (1992: 67) has described some of the key components of teacher development as relating to 'looking at teaching differently, seeing it in a new light, coming to appreciate its complexity more than we have done as yet'. This kind of process appears to me to be an entirely positive one which might well be triggered by working with a trainee. So, too, would be the (at first sight somewhat sad) outcome of 'possibl[y] develop[ing] a more hesitant manner, a kind of *pedagogical stammer*, as a result of our reflection and newly won insight' (ibid., emphasis added).

This kind of especially interesting argument was also advanced by Healy and Welchert (1990), who held that mentoring is fundamentally a *reciprocal* relationship, in which there are potential benefits for both mentor and trainee; it has the potential to be a 'transformative' experience for both. It is distinguishable 'from other superior/subordinate interactions', having for the trainee the object of 'the achievement of an identity transformation, a movement from the status of understudy to that of self-directing colleague', while for the mentor the relationship may be 'a vehicle for achieving midlife "generativity" . . . meaning a *transcendence of stagnating self-preoccupation*' (ibid.: 17, emphasis added).

Put simply, trainees derive professional learning from what mentors are passing on to them, but this interaction itself may lead to growth in mentors' own understanding of their professionality and their motivation – and self-esteem, in all probability. This last point was succinctly put by one of the respondents in a fairly recent study of mentors and their selection for the role: 'It helped to make me feel more valued' (Cunningham 2004: 276).

- As well as novel approaches to classroom practice, many recently qualified trainees will now be bringing with them a facility with ICT-derived learning materials, and even innovative pedagogies associated with ICT, from which many mentors may learn much of value. Can 'old dogs' learn new tricks? It will depend on their receptivity to these.

- The kinds of professional development opportunities that may stem from gaining experience as a mentor are not insignificant. These may include opportunities to contribute more extensively to staff training and development activities or to assume a fuller range of supervisory functions in college. At West Kent College, in promoting mentoring, the college has described it as being 'a valuable career development for staff hoping for career progression into roles where they can demonstrate their experience of working with staff in a supportive role and developing policy' (WKC 2004). Many mentors have found their experience to be seen as highly relevant by universities seeking to recruit new teacher trainers. (These kinds of themes, especially, are further developed in Chapter 8.)

Enhancing the quality of student learning

Fundamentally, what the activity of mentoring has as its end-product is the enhancement of the learning experience of college students. The person who has been supportively mentored will work more effectively, and with greater insight, as a result of the guidance he/she has received, and the ultimate beneficiaries of this will be his/her learners. The vision outlined in *Equipping Our Teachers for the Future* (2004) talks about the 'direct impact' which teacher training has right across the range of post-compulsory provision, including, for example:

- the key skills that underpin success in education, lifelong learning and personal development;
- the attainment levels of young people and their aspirations to enter higher education, and courses such as Foundation Degrees. (DfES 2004: 5)

Mentors can, rightly, accord themselves much credit in these contexts.

The 'learning professional'

I conclude this section simply by underlining the fact that certain of the above rewards serve to emphasise the ways in which mentor–trainee relations are not exclusively 'one way' relationships but are 'giving–taking' interactions. There can often be a rewarding mutuality in the exchange. In a number of respects it seems there is real potential for the professional learning that takes place within the setting of the mentoring relationship to apply to both parties. The interesting Guile and Lucas notion of a 'learning professional' (in Green and Lucas 1999) would appear to accommodate this process as one of the dimensions of professional life which takes us beyond reflective practice – at least in its 'minimalist', predominantly introspective and retrospective mode.

Similarly, according to Nicholls (2001) at least in higher education the professional identity of 'learning professionals' owes much to their *receptivity to ideas*. Such professionals show obvious capacities for listening to and learning from the communities they serve.

There is also in mentoring, it seems, scope for avoiding, as an established professional, the kind of disengagement or bitterness which Michael Huberman has reviewed in his work on teachers' life-spans (or 'life cycles'). With a commendable tentativeness, Huberman wonders whether mature teachers sometimes display a tendency to 'withdraw' – perhaps, citing Becker, because of frustrated ambitions or 'plateauing' in the profession. This kind of process may be about disengaging 'from policies and practices of which one disapproves . . . [or] a response to pressures from the environment to cede one's place to younger colleagues and fresher ideas' (Huberman 1992: 126).

Engaging in mentoring, one might argue, could militate against these negatives, and entail a degree of professional renewal – or at least achievement of the 'serenity' (ibid.: 127) which Huberman sees as an alternative to bitterness. For some readers, this kind of formulation may seem to somewhat over-dramatise what lies in store – negative or positive – for long-term teachers, but I would argue that the perspective is not all that difficult to connect with a discussion of reasons why mentoring might hold notable benefits for *mentors* as well as trainees.

The challenges

It would offer a 'straightforward' approach to summing up mentoring's challenges if one simply tried to categorise these as being either practical, professional or personal – such a beguiling, alliterative schema might indeed have its proponents. However, in reality, there are quite often very fuzzy lines between the ways in which mentors can experience a sense of being challenged. For example, the 'professional' challenge of managing a difficult post-observation debriefing can easily shade into the intensely personal one of having to attempt to 'switch off' after a sometimes extremely stressful event to allow for some kind of relatively untroubled home life. And, somewhere in most mentors' thinking, questions of *ethics* will at some stage arise – such questions can derive from any of the realms we might be tempted to separate out as being either practical, professional or personal.

The 'time-poor' mentor

Probably the easiest challenge to identify in the life of a mentor is simply finding *time* to engage in the activity. In an ideal world, mentors would all have been given a reduction in the amount of time they are required to be available for other duties (see Chapter 1's proposal to this effect). In general, colleges do not expect teachers to assume personal tutor responsibilities without formally structuring this activity into their timetable, and in certain regards a case could be made for the same sort of principle to apply to mentoring, as it does in some institutions.

Where the time demands of mentoring are not, however, formally acknowledged in this way it will call for a particularly skilled approach to time management, and real awareness of trainees' anxieties over not having enough time to discuss their concerns, and their developing practice, with mentors. Mentors may have to 'state the obvious' and spell out that they typically spend their days 'multi-tasking', with teaching, meetings, paperwork and, often, middle-management responsibilities competing with mentoring for their attention.

Trainees will not, certainly early on in the relationship, always connect automatically with just how busy a mentor may be; they may well need, for example, an explanation as to why a post-observation debriefing might have to take place at the end of a day rather than immediately after the end of a lesson (a situation such as will arise where a mentor first has two lessons of their own to teach, for instance).

A highly relevant aspect of the boundary setting advocated in this guide will be the necessity to frame, in advance of key meetings, the period it will be possible to allocate to them: 'We'll have roughly half an hour, if we start promptly at 4 o'clock, just after my own class ends.'

Role conflict

Mentors may be challenged by issues arising as a result of *role conflict*. This may well be especially likely where a trainee is failing to make satisfactory progress against targets that have been set for him/her. The principal reason role conflict may arise has much to do with a potential tension between mentors wishing to accentuate the nurturing, supportive dimensions of the role while at the same time needing to acknowledge their role in assuring high standards of learning and teaching. Mentors adhering to a strongly humanistic, Rogerian educational philosophy may be especially challenged. They are *assessing performance*, and so long as this function has to be carried out (see below) it will set certain limits on the extent to which they can allow the type and pace of a trainee's professional learning to be wholly self-determined.

In cases where mentors are beginning to have concerns about a trainee's progress they may be torn between wanting to 'give the benefit of the doubt' – to wait a while longer to see where improvements based on advice begin to be evident – and being aware that training institutions, typically, insist on the earliest possible reporting of such concerns. Should they 'send in the form' or not? This kind of scenario will be but one of the many which will challenge the professional judgement, and the overall professionalism, of mentors.

Official, i.e. institutional, endorsement of mentoring as an activity is most usually born out of a mixture of altruism and pragmatism on the part of college managers. The former stimulates a search for individuals whose approachability and good interpersonal skills can be seen as likely to give *trainees* the best experience they can hope for; the latter seeks experienced staff who will, first and foremost, see the quality of *student* learning, and achievement levels, as standing to gain most from the supportive work they will undertake with trainees.

As so often, the dichotomy here may, however, be a false one – a contented trainee who feels that his/her potential is being nurtured, and professional standards are developing, is not in some way a polar opposite of a group of learners who are achieving their educational aims. There is a convincing case for arguing that the two things are strongly interrelated. And mentors who are able to operate as *critical friends* are those most likely to strengthen and deepen the relationship between trainee development and learner achievement. In practical terms, being a critical friend entails balancing the kind of psychosocial support for a trainee (which probably leads them to describe a mentor's friendship and approachability) with being able to offer such criticism as is needed to ensure that college learners' achievements do not suffer as a result of exposure to habitually ineffective practice. Offering criticism *constructively* will not cause trainees to lose any professional respect or liking they may have shown towards a mentor.

It is understandable that mentors can experience certain tensions in the role – they can never, after all, be solely concerned with any one single focus, whether this be offering curriculum advice, organising a programme of classes for a trainee to teach, or whatever. These activities will always be found associated with evaluative functions, and those related to the assessment of practice. Cox, writing on 'teacher as mentor', draws attention to the 'tension *generated by the assessment function* of the mentor' (Cox 1996: 42, cited in Huddleston and Unwin 2002: 185, my emphasis). Cox was, in fact, arguing for a wider adoption of peer or collaborative mentoring to address what she saw as a problematic 'imbalance of power' (ibid.) and such arrangements as she suggests do have a number of positive benefits. However, within the specific context of the current training framework it is a fact that both mentors and trainees will need to continue to live with a degree of 'tension', and manage this as professionally as possible.

Ultimately, mentors under present statutory arrangements covering training for, and entry to, the profession of college teacher are also in a gatekeeping role to some extent. Some may find this a worrying realisation, but others may find it one which further enhances their professional self-esteem; playing a part in raising the quality of the teaching in colleges is a significant, and laudable, contribution.

Boundary setting

Mentors may be challenged by the need to try to set certain boundaries around the interaction they must have with their trainees. Some such boundaries will not need to be agonised over as they will be, to a large extent, specified by the structure and regulations of whatever training programme is being followed – 'How many hours per week must I ensure this person teaches?'; 'How many times per term must I observe them?'; 'What procedure must I follow if their attendance/punctuality record drops below X%?' All of these questions are likely to be susceptible to clear, easy-to-find answers. Other questions will, at first sight, have answers that are slightly fuzzier, and some of these will need to be negotiated with trainees. The issue of *mentor availability* has already been referred to, but is worth underlining as it causes so many grievances where trainees do not perceive that it has been made explicit by individual mentors just what is going to be feasible in terms of frequency/length/times of meetings. It is an area well worth clarifying at the earliest stage, taking pains to ensure that trainees understand and sympathise with the reasons why an offer may appear to be less generous than they might have been anticipating.

Communicating with trainees

Certain of the above boundaries are specifically to do with *communication*, and are of major significance. The modes in which mentor and trainee communicate with each other, and the purposes for which they communicate, will all need sensible discussion early on. For example, if mentors feel it will be efficient to allow trainees to have their personal phone numbers (so that they might, say, discuss any emergency cover arrangements necessitated by a trainee's illness), up to what time at night will it be acceptable to make contact? How 'routine' ought it to be that a trainee contacts a mentor at the weekend to talk through their ideas for lessons? If a trainee is to be invited to use e-mail to raise queries with their mentor, what kind of response time might they be advised of?

These are questions about which it is not that constructive for trainers, college managers or other parties to attempt to legislate on. They require case-by-case discussion between mentor and trainee, and the agreement of fair, manageable boundaries. If these are not arrived at, a lot of ill will on both sides can be generated.

Internal and external loci of control

The apparent difficulty some trainees have in accepting criticism (especially, but not only, when seeing it as 'destructive') was largely dealt with in connection with observations. However, a further idea that is worth touching on here can be related to such difficulties when they seem to arise for a trainee over *any* issues raised with them. Such issues might, for example, be to do with such matters as poor attendance at team meetings ('No one ever informs me about these') or routinely causing student complaints by returning their marked work late ('But most of them give it in late anyway'). Mentors – should we need to remind ourselves – are responsible for supporting trainees in every aspect of their developing professionalism, not just their classroom competence. They are thus exposed to the stresses and strains of possibly having to make criticisms of any one of a number of dimensions of a trainee's performance within an institution. For this reason it may, in some respects, be helpful to have recourse to a possible explanation of quite why it is that some trainees 'handle' such criticisms so poorly.

The trainee who appears incapable of ever accepting that the responsibility for some aspect of their underperformance must rest with them alone is often an extremely challenging individual with whom to work, always citing reasons 'beyond their control' for why things are going wrong. Probably every reader of this guide will be able to recognise this person. On the other hand, mentors may work with trainees who are usually far less challenging because they will acknowledge their own part in events and do not claim passive victimhood.

The contrasts between such trainees may sometimes be explicable in terms of their having either an internal *locus of control* or one which is external. As will probably already have been surmised from the terminology used here, it is the trainee in whose responses to criticism (and to events in general) there is 'an absence of self' who is operating with an *external* locus of control. The course of events in their view is determined wholly by factors external to themselves. Therefore they are liable to ask, for instance, 'What could I do about *that*?' and are also likely to dismiss most answers to the question as being unworkable in one way or another. Far less stressful for mentors are the trainees who seem able to discern *in themselves* an appropriate degree of responsibility for something which has (or hasn't) taken place. The internal locus of control possessed by such individuals allows them to see that they are *not* powerless to influence the course of events. These, then, are the trainees who will most readily take responsibility for effecting improvements in their professional behaviours.

Letting go

For what are often the most positive, supportive, motives imaginable, mentors may sometimes simply take far too much upon themselves when they work with trainees (as they may have already displayed a tendency to do in their work with college learners or their personal tutees). Most trainees require a lot of 'hand-holding' in the early stages of a mentoring relationship, and weaker trainees will take longer than others to wean off a highly intensive process which makes great demands on mentors' time and energies. However, what is important is to articulate at a point in the relationship judged by the mentor to be most appropriate that the frequency/intensity of contact will be diminishing, that the degree of monitoring (e.g. of lesson plans, learning materials etc.) will be less and that, crucially, the trainee's professional autonomy will be what benefits most from these shifts in the preoccupations of the mentoring relationship.

It is extremely hard to avoid creating *overdependence* in trainees if mentors do not make real efforts to scale down their supportive interventions. It is very protective of trainees – and therefore not, of course, a malignant thing – to want to continually be on hand for them, to be a sounding-board for lesson ideas, to closely monitor how the challenges of classroom management are being met, and so on. Yet, for most practical purposes, they will lead a profoundly *un*protected life once qualified and will probably be best prepared for this by a phased reduction in access to a mentor – by mentors 'letting go' in stages.

One of the devices that may prove of assistance in the 'letting go' process is an extremely straightforward one: it is simply to step up the degree of *praise* which is being given towards the end of the mentoring relationship. Clearly, I cannot advocate providing *unfounded* praise, but wherever possible, praising should be a strong element of instilling in trainees the confidence to fit their professional identities as new teachers. The kinds of 'signing off' statements which my own trainees have said were of high value in this context include:

- 'You have a very good grasp of different students' needs. It sometimes takes teachers years to get this.'

- 'I have learnt more from you this year than you have learnt from me.'

- 'You have done your best, far beyond what's expected of you – it's up to the students now.'

- 'You bring a breath of fresh air into teaching and the department as a whole.'

- 'Teaching students with learning difficulties is definitely your calling.'

- '. . . work your magic.'

References

Cunningham, B. (2004) 'Some have mentoring thrust upon them: the element of choice in mentoring in PCET environments'. *Research in Post-Compulsory Education*, 9(2), 271–82.

DfES (2004) *Equipping Our Teachers for the Future: Reforming Initial Teacher Training for the Learning and Skills Sector*. Nottingham: Department for Education and Skills.

Green, A. and Lucas, N. (1999) *FE and Lifelong Learning: Realigning the Sector for the Twenty-first Century*. London: Bedford Way Papers, Institute of Education, University of London.

Healy, C. C. and Welchert, A. J. (1990) 'Mentoring relations: a definition to advance research and practice'. *Educational Researcher*, 19(9), 17–21.

Huberman, M. (1992) 'Teacher development and instructional mastery', in Hargreaves, A. and Fullan, M. G. *Understanding Teacher Development*. New York: Teachers College Press.

Huddleston, P. and Unwin, L. (2002) *Teaching and Learning in Further Education* (2nd edn). London: RoutledgeFalmer.

McKelvey, C. and Andrews, J. (1998) 'Why do they do it? A study into the perceptions and motivations of trainee further education lecturers'. *Research in Post-Compulsory Education*, 3(3), 357–67.

Nicholls, G. (2001) *Professional Development in Higher Education.* London: Kogan Page.

WKC (2004) *Mentoring Policy.* Tonbridge: West Kent College.

6

Problem-focused mentoring and working with other mentors

Chapter objectives:

- To review ways in which mentoring may need to incorporate strongly 'remedial' components and may benefit from collaborative approaches (both formal and informal) in cases of trainees' underperformance.
- To examine some aspects of trainee failure and the lessons which may be learnt from this phenomenon.

What I endeavour to do in this chapter is show ways in which, especially where problems are arising over a trainee's progress, collaborating with mentors (and sometimes other key staff) may be advantageous. Arguments, or at least reservations, will obviously present themselves as to the feasibility of such collaboration given the ever-increasing demands being made on mentors' time and energies. Nevertheless, working with others does appear to be an aspect of mentoring that deserves contemplation because of its great potential benefits to both mentors and trainees.

Rationale for working with other mentors

At first sight, mentoring may appear to be an activity solely dependent for its success on a close one-to-one relationship, and the greatest part of the time spent on the task of mentoring a trainee teacher will indeed be spent in this setting. However, where problems are beginning to arise with a trainee there may well be notable advantages to adopting a collegial approach to these. Where mentors are based in an institution hosting a number of trainees, or employing teachers, some of whom are concurrently undergoing training, then in general there will be at least a few staff engaged in mentoring. Teaching can, for much of the time seem, paradoxically, quite a lonely profession, as observed by writers such as Hargreaves and Fullan (1992). I would claim that this perspective holds good for mentoring, and suggest that it is therefore probably a worthwhile counter to such feelings to engage in the types of collegial exchange being suggested in this section.

Distributed mentoring

As well as promoting collegiality with other mentors I would also point to the benefits of networking with a wider cross-section of practitioners within a college. The participation which trainees themselves engage in is, in reality, far more complex than that of their dyadic relationship with their mentor. I am not referring here merely to their relationships with learners, but with their circle of colleagues; some of these may, *de facto*, be functioning as additional mentors, so numerous are their interventions (both supportive and otherwise). This kind of consideration perhaps applies most strongly when we examine the position of full-time trainees, only attending an institution on a teaching practice placement basis. Such trainees very frequently report that they have received valuable guidance from teachers whose classes they have been covering, for example – and often (in the case of specialists such as those in Art and Design or the sciences) from technicians as well.

The kind of situation described here may equate the *distributed mentoring* within communities of practice which Pare and Le Maistre (2004) observed. This does not in any way undermine an officially designated mentor's role (although in certain circumstances it is conceivable that it might do so, where messages relating to aspects of practice are decidedly mixed ones). Nor is acknowledging the probability of 'distributed mentoring' existing the same as advocating some kind of 'just ask anyone' culture. A trainee's contact with the kinds of individuals mentioned is more often than not of a type that will only further accelerate their professional learning, and for this reason some mentors may actively promote it. Some trainees will, more proactively than others, seek out additional support, intuitively identifying colleagues who may be most receptive to requests for additional guidance. From experience, it also appears to be the case that 'distributed mentoring' takes place simply because many college staff are so supportive and happy to take trainees 'under their wing'. This seems to apply most strongly where such staff perceive that the official mentor is someone with an especially onerous range of responsibilities who is perhaps struggling to meet a trainee's entitlements in terms of regular contact.

Where it is evident to mentors that others have been working supportively with their trainee then it is only sensible to liaise with the individuals concerned. This will allow for more efficient monitoring of the trainee's concerns and of their developing practice. It will also militate against the possibility of the mixed messages alluded to above, and the needless repetition of points – although, of course, it is hardly a disaster if a trainee hears important ideas reiterated, and thereby learns that there may be some kind of professional consensus on certain issues.

Opportunities might, though, also present themselves in colleges for sharing concerns, either informally or formally, with others, with the intention of drawing on a larger potential pool of experience and professional understandings than one mentor alone can hope to possess. There are certainly important issues to bear in mind here, including the very straightforward one concerning time pressures, or finding ourselves to be 'time poor' as it has been sometimes expressed of late. There is obviously going to be a measure of difficulty attached to ever finding good points in the working week when any group of college teachers can come together to discuss matters relating to teacher training.

Clearly, also, it has to be acknowledged that there are potentially serious hazards associated with confidentiality and trust – or rather breaches of these – where trainees, especially those seen as 'underperforming', are being discussed. It is essential, and beneficial to all parties, if mentors, who as a group decide to occasionally work together in college to try to solve problems, make this fact explicit to trainees, managers and the relevant certificate-awarding institution. Mentors should not involve themselves in any activity that carries the slightest risk of being construed as 'talking behind someone's back'. The fact that mentors may meet together as a group to discuss the progress of individual trainees should be out in the open, and the rationale for doing so articulated clearly.

Action learning sets

In a number of professional contexts, a valuable framework for professional learning and problem-solving may exist in the form of 'action learning', and in particular the notion of the 'action learning set'. This will now be briefly outlined to enable mentors to decide whether it has the potential to support their work, especially in the context of trainees who are at risk of not succeeding on their programme.

It is possible to critique the proposal that participating in action learning be integrated within any formally *required* dimensions of a mentor's role. The nature of the exercise, and its time demands, means that a number of mentors could well perceive it as entirely unrealistic that they engage with a commitment to an action learning set. However, it seems at least worth indicating what is entailed and what professional benefits may be derived from action learning as a mechanism for linking *reflection* on practice with *action* to improve practice.

A very highly regarded guide to the scope and purposes of action learning in professional settings is that written by Ian McGill and Liz Beaty, first published in 1992. The authors describe

> a continuous process of learning and reflection, supported by colleagues, with an intention of getting things done. Through action learning individuals learn with and from each other by working on real problems and reflecting on their own experiences.
>
> (McGill and Beaty 2001: 11)

Working with a group of colleagues, called the 'set', 'the individual . . . comes to the set to learn from experience and to move on to more effective action'. How this process may look in practice can be briefly summarised as follows.

A small group – ideally no more than six or seven – will arrange to come together to form a 'set'.

- The set will generate ground rules for its operation, including such matters as length and frequency of meetings, and confidentiality within the set.
- The set members will each bring an issue or concern with which they would value guidance and support.
- Agreement is reached within the set regarding whose issue should be worked on first, and over how many meetings; an allocation of time is agreed on, representing the entitlement [my own term] of each set member.
- The set works in a wholly focused way on the problem presented by one member, enhancing reflection on the nature of the problem, and attempting to arrive at some concrete proposals for action.
- The process of action learning then entails moving on to allow a second set member to present their issue, and benefit from the set's reflections and ideas for action; and so on, over the life of the set.

As will, I hope, be evident, the action learning set is thus a powerful tool for professional learning and action in that individual set members are able to draw on the insights of others. Sometimes these will be merely endorsing and giving a legitimacy to ideas for action that the member may already have been intuitively moving towards, but this in itself can be seen as of high value.

The 'set' is a formal entity, working to clear rules and within stated boundaries. What it ought to be based on, however, are very human, and humanistic, qualities – some of which were alluded to when dealing with mentor attributes much earlier on in this guide. Set members need to experience feelings of mutual professional regard, of trust and of openness. It will not be possible for the set to accomplish much of value if members are guarded about sharing their problems because they fear being viewed as inadequate or not coping with their role in teacher training.

Sets work best in an atmosphere of trust where members feel able to disclose their feelings and thoughts to others *without judgement* and in confidence. Lack of trust can render the set impotent as individuals are unlikely to focus on real and important issues where they feel they will be ridiculed or that others will discuss their issue outside the set. (ibid.: 54, emphasis added)

Set members need to be able to ask for what they need from the set, and to be able to deal with questioning aimed at getting them to see, or reframe, their particular issue using other perspectives. No issue should be diminished in its importance; if it has been brought to the set it must be approached as meriting serious consideration. In terms of language use within the set, phrases such as 'I just don't see what the problem is' or 'I can't see why you're worrying about it' are likely to have negative results, and even to jeopardise the existence of the set. As with the work you will carry out with your trainee, a cautious self-monitoring of your language use will be well worth striving for.

Certain of the considerations described above, for example the need to try to avoid language use with judgemental overtones, will clearly apply with equal strength to informal relations with other mentors in an institution. The onus on us all to demonstrate consideration and empathy with colleagues who may be experiencing professional challenges is not exclusive to the special nature of action learning sets.

It is, finally, worth alluding to the possibility that working as a set member may be found to be such a positive, empowering manifestation of collegiality that mentors may actively consider adopting this approach to problem-solving in contexts unrelated to initial teacher training. It may, at the very least, be that the perceived beneficial effects on mentors' interpersonal skills deriving from set membership will be long-lasting ones and that this fact in itself makes having been involved in action learning a positive experience. The way of working in this context potentially has valuable 'spin offs' into many dimensions of our professional and personal lives:

Few of us live and work in isolation; so much of our experience in work and life rests upon being effective in the presence of and with other people. Having knowledge about something may be useless if we cannot convey, act, interrelate, in a manner that is effective for the purpose. (ibid.: 118)

It is, therefore, hoped that this extremely brief 'taster' of what action learning may facilitate in the context of mentoring might stimulate an exploration of its potential in other areas. A variation on the theme of action learning involves the use of on-line methods, where mentors may post questions/outline scenarios. Here, what modernity offers is a greater degree of flexibility over the 'where and when' of exchanges between mentors – although perhaps we lose something crucially important in moving away from face-to-face contact.

Networking with the trainers

Universities will often provide a forum for the sharing both of best practice and difficulties experienced in supporting trainees. However, these will typically be on an extremely occasional basis, even if it is arguable that they should be a far more regular feature of partnership arrangements. Some university-based training schemes simply seem more successful than others at enticing mentors to be actively involved with their in-house events, but here I would only encourage mentors to participate in such advertised events wherever possible. The opportunities to network with mentors from other PCET institutions, and learn something of how mentoring operates across a range of these, is well worthwhile. It is also worth remembering that the agenda for such events is not always that rigid, and some professional 'guerilla activity' in steering trainers into a focus on the issues which are most exercising mentors may well pay off.

Liaising with trainees' tutors

Even where mentors' other commitments preclude actually attending such mentoring-related off-site events as are available, other mechanisms for contact with trainers, and most especially personal tutors, are in place and need to be used.

Whether mentors are working with a full-time or part-time trainee they will have a tutor responsible for their overall progress on their PGCE or CertEd course. This person will often make themselves known at the college/department quite early on and will have provided their phone/e-mail contact details. They will be involved, as mentors will, with the observation of trainees' practical teaching and will read mentors' (and others') observation and synoptic reports. It is this individual with whom it is absolutely essential to keep in close touch, most especially when it begins to seem as if all is not well with the trainee's performance. 'Performance' is used here to reiterate that what is observable both in and outside of a trainee's classes should be reported on. It will be of equal interest to a tutor to learn about matters such as commitment to key aspects of college life as attending meetings, staffing open evenings and advice sessions, assisting with departmental resources etc. Clearly, trainees who are also college employees will be primarily within the jurisdiction of relevant managers within the organisation, though in terms of 'taking action' on underperformance in the kinds of areas mentioned here, it will be the college and not the awarding institution (where they are not one and the same) that must decide how to proceed.

One essential point to note in the above contexts is that, however inflexible this may appear, there will almost inevitably be requirements placed on mentors to use certain documentation in their correspondence/reporting both to trainees and trainers. It is not at all unheard of to illustrate this point for a training institution that wishes to withhold certification from a trainee to be successfully challenged over this purely because an observation report was written on plain paper, and/or where a mentor entered their comments under a set of subheadings which were not 100 per cent aligned with the official ones.

From dyad to triad

Two specific, highly practical ways in which mentors and trainees' tutors can usefully work together are in the, usually related, contexts of:

- the three-way meeting with a trainee; and
- the co-observation of practical teaching.

In both of these, what occurs is that the normally dyadic relationship between mentor and trainee becomes momentarily a triadic one. The principal advantage of this, as I hope will be made clear, is that of being able to triangulate the views of mentor and tutor, so that the risk of subjective judgements regarding trainee performance is reduced.

For example, if both mentor and tutor co-observe a trainee's class, this will simply allow them to compare notes and provide a balanced analysis of a session's strengths, and – what is likely to be of more interest if such an event has been organised – its weaknesses. Has either the mentor or the tutor adopted an idiosyncratic, overly critical view of some aspects of the session, or would both agree that something has been problematic?

The kind of three-way meeting involving mentor, tutor and trainee which I have been involved in has taken the form of either a post-observation *debriefing*, as alluded to above, or a *synoptic review* of progress and problems. Neither of these are the easiest events to arrange, given our crowded professional lives, but almost always have useful outcomes. For instance, trainees' perceptions that 'it's just the mentor/tutor who doesn't like me' can be ameliorated in such a setting if agreement does emerge on the part of both of the responsible individuals that certain things offer scope for improvement. Sometimes it may even lead trainees to feel that they are seen as important enough to cause two busy professionals to expend extra time and effort working with them.

On the other hand, having to teach a class with two observers present, rather than just one, is extremely stressful for some trainees – and may even pull down their performance further. And the experience of the three-way meeting may feel to a trainee like being 'ganged up on'. Both situations need especially skilful presentation and handling; the *rationale* for both needs to be made exceptionally clear, and the potentially positive benefits need to be stressed. The key mentor – and trainer – attribute of being able to empathise will come to the fore, alongside the management of such practicalities as unthreatening room arrangements, as far as the three-way meeting is concerned.

References

Hargreaves, A. and Fullan, M. G. (1992) *Understanding Teacher Development.* New York: Teachers College Press.

McGill, I. and Beaty, L. (2001) *Action Learning: A Guide for Professional, Management and Educational Development.* London: Kogan Page.

Pare, A. and LeMaistre, C. (2004) 'Learning through complex participation: distributed mentoring in communities of practice', in Tynjala, P., Valiman, J. and Boulton-Lewis, G. (eds) *Higher Education and Working Life: Collaborations, Confrontations and Challenges.*

Case studies and critical incidents in mentoring

Chapter objective:

- To examine the merits of two discrete, but clearly interrelated, perspectives on professional learning, focusing on their role within mentoring.

Case studies in mentoring

> The tendency to promote stories of happy endings is hardly surprising, for who would wish (or dare) to wash any dirty linen about unproductive or failed relationships in public, let alone define such failures as mentoring? (Colley 2003)

Helen Colley is no doubt correct in pointing to the way in which the benefits – the positive outcomes – of the activity of mentoring are those that tend to be accentuated. It would be dispiriting in the extreme to spend any significant amount of time dissecting ways in which mentoring relationships may fail, and my own preoccupation in this guide has been to try to promote and celebrate the value of mentors' work. Nevertheless, it seems both worthwhile and realistic to at least include reference in what follows to one less-than-successful mentoring relationship by way of a 'cautionary tale', and with an exceptionally high degree of anonymity having been introduced when depicting the relationship between mentor and trainee. The main emphasis of this section is indeed, though, to illustrate how 'happy endings' have been arrived at.

The case studies that follow are presented in the form of three first-person 'testimonies', these having been supplied by recently qualified new entrants. I have only amended the originals in any way where I judged that there was a serious risk of mentors being able to identify themselves or the trainee (although, in fact, one of the mentors especially would seem to have much to be proud of in their practice). Following each of the three case studies I have indicated what some of the key issues in the narratives – both positive and negative – appear to be, although I am aware that some readers might perhaps judge this to have been superfluous. Each of the trainees followed a full-time pre-service PGCE course, so none was at the time employed in their colleges.

The first 'testimony' seems to offer a particularly interesting case study in that the author – a quite outstanding teacher, even as a trainee – has subsequently become a highly effective mentor and teacher trainer.

CASE STUDY 1

While I was doing my PGCE I read a book on mentoring, and although I don't remember much about it I do remember that the author recommended that mentors should spend 70 minutes a week with their student teachers. The reason why this figure stuck in my mind was because it seemed such a huge length of time, given that I spent on average (over the year) about a couple of minutes a week with my mentor.

According to the Institute my mentor was supposed to guide and to instruct me in terms of college administration, health and safety, and pastoral aspects of education; she was supposed to inform me about the curriculum, the students and their work, about issues of classroom management and so on. However, my mentor didn't seem to have read the guidebook on effective mentoring, or if she had, she had taken to heart the bit about not being over-protective.

At the start I saw her quite regularly, as she arranged which lessons I should observe. After the first week, however, I was left to take the initiative and to approach teachers so that I could watch a variety of lessons (from Key Skills to A Level), and more importantly, perhaps, a range of teaching styles, methods and strategies.

It didn't seem long after that that I was being approached to cover lessons. One instance I remember vividly was where a teacher had been on holiday over the half-term break and quite clearly couldn't face teaching first thing on Monday morning. There was clearly no supervision going on here and at no point did I ever teach with another teacher in the room. Being a relatively experienced teacher, I didn't mind this too much, but what I *would* have liked was some time to talk about teaching strategies with her (about successful methods she had used to teach a particular class/student/text; about effective teaching strategies and activities that she had seen other teachers use etc.).

What she *did* do was to plan my initial observations of other teachers (albeit for a brief period); she did organise my teaching timetable (although this became increasingly *ad hoc*), and we did have a couple of planned meetings during the year (these were generally strategic sessions in which we discussed my timetable.)

Therefore, while her planning, liaising and guiding may have been somewhat lacking, and she clearly believed in the hit-and-miss, pick-it-up-as-you-go-along style of mentoring, in terms of teaching she did lead by example. She was a good teacher, with an excellent classroom manner and with finely honed classroom management skills. In her observation of my lesson, too, she was thorough and constructive.

In retrospect, I can see that the reason for her 'hands-off' approach to mentoring was not that she had no regard for the post or for me. The reasons were more complicated than this. I suspect that I did not ask enough of her, and was flattered to think that she felt I was sufficiently competent take the initiative, to plan and to run classes myself. I also think that her incentive for being a dedicated mentor seemed to have shrunk to the fact that she could put it on her CV. Being a good mentor lies partly in a successful relationship between the university, the college and the teacher him/herself. If the support is lacking from either the university or the college, the teacher's motivation has to be intrinsic. The college at which I worked received money for each student teacher that they took on, but none of that money seemed to be translated into either pay or relief hours for the mentors. If I had known that relief hours had been awarded to my mentor, the whole system of meeting, planning etc. could have been more structured, with an allotted discussion time set for each week.

In the years following my PGCE I have mentored many student teachers. It has only been by doing this that I have discovered just how many different roles and jobs a successful mentor has, and just how difficult (without relief hours) it is to find 70 minutes a week in a busy teaching timetable.

The above account teaches us a good deal, beginning with the way in which the trainee had discerned that a guidance handbook supplied to the mentor had not been read. But there is, of course, a real awareness, gained through subsequent mentoring/training, of the challenges caused by insufficient *time* to mentor. There are also some interesting pointers to the way in which a balance needs to be struck between 'hands-off' approaches (for which one might sometimes read 'too much autonomy too soon') and the need to provide adequate guidance on teaching at an early stage.

By way of a much different perspective on the experience of being mentored, one which was, at times, so demotivating as to have almost caused the trainee to withdraw from her programme, what follows contains some important lessons for us all.

When I began my PGCE I was hopeful for the future and excited and full of enthusiasm to start my teaching placement practice, which would hopefully lead me further towards the change of career I had chosen for myself. I enjoyed the first two weeks of the course at my university and was not put off too much by the coursework or the academic demands of the course. Although nervous, I was hopeful that I would come to enjoy, or at least relish, the challenges that my placement would present. Although I didn't feel quite as confident about my teaching skills in practice, I was hopeful that with support and guidance from my mentor along the way I would soon be able to develop the skills necessary to be able to teach effectively in the classroom environment and to build on any existing skills I had acquired in previous teaching roles within the caring profession, where I had had nearly 20 years' working experience.

Eventually I was given a contact name for my mentor; but despite my efforts to contact him I did not eventually get to meet my mentor until the placement started, during one of the induction sessions. I met him briefly and we arranged to meet the next week when the placement started officially. When we did meet the following week it was very brief, and although I suggested having regular meetings during the placement for progress updates, which was agreed to, in the end only the minimum number of meetings were held throughout the placement.

I was invited to attend only one of my mentor's lessons during the first term to observe, prior to starting my own teaching practice, and very few other teachers at the college seemed willing to be observed within my department, although there were a few exceptions to whom I am most grateful, but they did not include my mentor. He did not attend or observe any of my taught lessons at all during my first term, and I generally had fleeting glimpses of him throughout the whole placement, when he would dash in and out of the staffroom between lessons or meetings, ask if I was OK and then dash out of the room again, barely stopping long enough to hear my reply.

It seemed that my mentor found out about my progress by asking other staff how I was coping; he did not come to see me teach a class until the middle of the second term of the placement, and gave me no feedback at all on my teaching practice until *after* my first formally assessed observation (which he failed to conduct himself, asking the placement co-ordinator to observe in his place). After the (very negative) feedback from this, I felt very disappointed and humiliated by the whole experience, since this was the first proper feedback I had received on my teaching practice since the start of the placement; and I was very angry, particularly with my mentor, that I had got so far in my placement without either he or anyone else having spoken to me about any problems with either my teaching methods or my classroom management abilities; so that I had no way of knowing until that stage that there were aspects of my teaching style that were, in the college's view, unsatisfactory.

I knew I was not the most experienced teacher in the classroom, and therefore was keen to have regular progress reports and welcomed any constructive criticism of my performance in class; but I did spend time planning my lessons meticulously and had shown the lesson plans to the subject tutor as well as to my mentor, who had had plenty of opportunity to advise me of any problems prior to either of my placement or training college observed assessments.

I felt very much as if I had been set up to fail by the staff at my placement college, and particularly by my mentor. I had some quite challenging classes to teach during my placement, and eventually, toward the middle of the spring term, after finally deciding I no longer had any confidence in my mentor, I decided to consult my personal tutor about my concerns regarding my progress on the placement and the absence of support and advice from my mentor. Following his intervention and a three-way meeting with the college placement co-ordinator, I went away for the Easter break feeling a little more reassured and hopeful that things would improve for the final term of the placement.

In the final term I returned to the college determined to finish the placement as best I could and to complete all the required teaching hours and reports that were required of me to satisfy my training institution, and hopefully to complete my final observed assessment with a reasonable grade. Fortunately, I managed to achieve all these things by the end of the placement.

But I left my placement college with my confidence in myself as a newly qualified teacher badly undermined by my experiences there. I felt that I hadn't been given a very well balanced insight into what classroom teaching involved, and disappointed that I had not been given a chance to grow and develop the skills as a beginner teacher in the way that I had hoped I would be able to do at the beginning of the course. Mostly, I felt saddened and disappointed that I seemed to have lost some confidence and some of the optimism and enthusiasm for teaching that I had started the course with; and on reflection, since my course ended, I can only conclude that the reason for this was entirely related to the lack of effective mentoring provided by my placement college during my training.

This somewhat dispiriting testimony truly underscores how the crucial importance of effective mentoring is probably best proven where it is *not* the experience of the trainee. With considerable attention being paid to salvaging something of the trainee's self-confidence, she was, however, subsequently able to contemplate applying for teaching positions. A number of negatives appear to have come into play here, including the fact the mentor had delegated the observation of an important, formally assessed, session without the trainee having been made aware of the reasons, which may have been legitimate ones.

The last of this small set of 'testimonies' returns us to a far more positive situation, one where the happy outcome was actually the appointment of the trainee to a college's successful Film and Media team.

CASE STUDY 3

I didn't have a huge amount of expectations to begin with, and wasn't entirely sure what exactly to expect from a mentor. I suppose I naïvely hoped for someone who would explain the dos and don'ts of teaching, alongside an idea of the college rules; someone who would be a link between the PGCE and the placement college.

In sight of this particular expectation, I also didn't think that a mentor would have teaching commitments. I had hoped for someone who would provide me with perfect textbook answers to my questions, while reinforcing the content of the PGCE. I also hoped for compassion and support.

What I got was far better than all that; my mentor gave me an optimistic yet realistic insight into teaching, consistent support, while providing encouragement and valuable feedback regarding my teaching practice.

I wasn't patronised and made to feel like the 'inadequate student teacher' that needs to learn everything. Instead my existing subject knowledge was brought onto courses, and I was encouraged to use what I know in innovative and creative ways in the classroom. I was taken on as 'the production person' in the department.

Praise was given, as well as constructive criticism, and a well-balanced approach towards my progress prompted me to address all feedback. Motivation was provided through different methods, such as allowing me to integrate subject areas that I was particularly interested in into lessons/handouts.

Ideas that worked were openly praised, re-used and borrowed by other teachers in the department, making me feel like a valued and appreciated member of the team.

My mentor always had time for me, even if her own workload was ridiculously high. She had provided me with her contact details and I was able to contact her at home if there were any issues that I was particularly worried about or wanted to discuss.

We also had regular meeting slots in which we discussed my feelings regarding progress so far, concerns etc. If I had nothing to discuss in relation to this, then we would lesson-plan or discuss handout designs for future sessions. The meetings used to last 20–40 minutes and I found them immensely useful.

If I made a mess of things or had a particularly horrible lesson, I was initially supported and provided with a positive spin on the situation. The situation was then later discussed when things had cooled down, or I had things more in perspective, and constructive criticism alongside effective strategies to explore were discussed. I found this approach sensitive, both boosting morale and motivation while allowing me to address the issue(s).

My mentor really mentored me. I know that sounds silly, but she really provided an immense level of support. And this support was consistent for the duration of my placement.

This account contains a number of interesting observations, but one of the *most* interesting seems to concern the steps which were taken by the mentor to *integrate* the trainee – a clear role is found for her in the host department which both exploits her pre-existing skills (to the department's benefit) and boosts her confidence. Another key dimension of the relationship between trainee and mentor is that there appears to have been an especially non-censorious attitude on the part of the latter when things didn't go well.

All three of these narratives seem to point to the high level of *expectations* trainees have of mentors, and to the pressing need to use any induction period to make absolutely clear what some of the boundaries, and constraints, of the mentoring relationship are likely to be at the local level, i.e. within a specific department/college.

Mentors might usefully collate their own set of case studies, and (with the appropriate anonymisation) share these with trainees. Each case study will throw up its own unique features, positive or negative, or a mixture of both, but from these there will be important lessons to be drawn. The case studies could be susceptible to incorporation in the kind of *professional development record* described in Chapter 8 – most especially where they provide clear evidence of effective mentoring raising trainee performance.

Critical incidents in mentoring

Any one of the three trainees who have provided the testimonies above might, with hindsight, describe one of the events they recount as constituting a *critical incident* in their development as teachers. A critical incident can be viewed as an event in one's professional life that has special significance for one or more reasons. For example:

- it may have involved being unprepared, to a very unsettling degree, to deal with a problem which arose;
- it caused a disturbance of equilibrium;
- it took the form of a dilemma, ethical or otherwise;
- it can be seen to have led to a lasting change in professional behaviour, principles or perceptions;
- it has caused continuing reflections over a substantial period – one keeps revisiting the incident, seeing more of its nature and implications on each occasion when its details are recalled; or
- it may have had major practical outcomes (including entering, or leaving, teaching).

Critical incidents as a component of professional learning are being used analytically within fields such as medicine, nursing and social work. The 'life or death' nature of many of the professional decisions made in such occupations could probably be cited by way of explanation for their adoption of critical incidents as a tool. Teachers, too, must make numerous decisions of importance in each working day, and are responsible – usually in teams – for the development and successes of their learners. And when things go seriously wrong in classrooms the lasting effects may well also have long-term – perhaps even lifelong – consequences.

It is hoped, therefore, that mentors will find something of value in a brief examination of the nature of critical incidents. It is possible to apply the idea to (a) the early professional development of mentored trainees (in particular their growing understanding of the nature of effective teaching); and (b) the continuing professional learning, *about mentoring*, of mentors themselves. David Tripp's (1993) book *Critical Incidents in Teaching* (sadly out of print at the time of writing) is a key resource for mentors who would like to explore this area in more depth, but is strongly rooted in the systems and cultures of schools rather than colleges. Mentors skilfully engaging in discussions of critical incidents with trainees, and also openly discussing their own critical incidents with peers, will undoubtedly be extending both their trainee's and their own repertoire of mentoring skills.

A valuable starting point is for mentors, having gained a basic understanding themselves of what is involved in critical incident analysis, to induct trainees into the benefits of this approach to reflective practice. Key points will be to ensure trainees appreciate that:

- almost by definition, not all incidents can possibly be critical;
- the 'criticality' of an incident may not be immediately evident – in general, a period of reflection will be needed before its status can be discerned;
- there is a range of possible settings in which critical incidents can be experienced – a classroom's walls are not what limits the potential for critical incidents to occur;
- while negativity – e.g. stress, hurt feelings or anger – may often characterise an incident, its underlying nature can be positive in terms of its influence on professional development.

Virtually all teacher trainees, whether on pre- or in-service programmes, have been required for some time now to maintain *reflective logs* or *journals*. Unless a training provider explicitly bars such a modification, mentors could encourage their trainees to include a section specifically titled 'Critical Incident Log'. Entries in this can be discussed in mentor–trainee meetings, or where a group of trainees is based in an institution they could be shared within the wider forum that is thus possible. Critical incident workshops can even be organised, to allow for the fullest possible exploration of any key professional themes that emerge from trainees' experiences.

There are, of course, risks associated with adopting a 'critical incidents' framework in the mentoring of early career professionals. One of these is to reiterate the point that *not* all incidents can possibly be critical. On a week-by-week basis, trainees will be experiencing a great number of professional interactions with learners, colleagues, support staff and mentors, and very few of these indeed will have a dramatic impact on their practice. At the end of a term, however, it might well be that some of this interaction can be seen to have a larger significance – and one or two elements might indeed possess a criticality in terms of how they have sharpened the reflective process, or actually triggered a change in practice. Similarly, not all the mistakes made by trainees in their classes will be that unsettling (for either learners or trainees themselves) and the professional learning stimulated by such mistakes will be of significance only on the microscale. For example, it may be embarrassing for someone to realise they have inadvertently placed an OHT on the projector upside down – it may get a laugh, perhaps, from a group, but it is not indicative of any major failure to understand the purpose of employing such a basic aid to teaching.

By contrast, however, a trainee being approached by a learner group's representative with a complaint that his/her teaching seems to largely comprise displaying/talking over OHTs, the entire contents of which have to be noted down, *is* the type of exchange – especially if it is clear that it deals with an issue which has been festering for some time – that will cause very serious, critical reflection on how the job of classroom teaching is being approached. Why has the trainee been using one method in preference to all others? Have the merits of variation of approach not been adequately considered? What has been going so wrong in the relationship with a learner group that such a crucially important piece of feedback has not been given much earlier? For all these reasons – and probably others which readers will conceive of – there appears to be a *critical* difference between what the trainee has been receiving here and what is described above.

The second important risk attached to the use of critical incidents with trainees is that the device can be accused (as reflective practice itself sometimes is) of being too backward-looking, fruitlessly introspective and limiting. The phrase 'navel-gazing' is one often used by critics of reflection in professional development – and perhaps sometimes this harsh perspective may have been justified. Yet the whole point of critical incidents – and here we might usefully recourse to the *OED* – is that they mark 'a point at which some action, property or condition *passes over into another*' (my italics). In other words, it is the trans-formational potential of critical incidents to which attention needs to be drawn – they allow a focus on the 'before', but far more importantly cause us to look towards the 'after'. If we have accepted a claim for mentoring as being a *trans-formative* set of actions, as well as simply supportive ones, a corollary is that it becomes much easier to acknowledge and celebrate the developmental nature of reflection in general and critical incidents in particular.

It is, as indicated, important to raise trainees' awareness of the great diversity of settings in which the origins of critical incidents may lie. Some examples of such settings, besides classrooms, are given below.

Settings where there is the potential for critical incidents to occur:

1. Another teacher's classroom (possibly the mentor's), in which a trainee is conducting an observation.
2. The debriefing room, when discussing a recent observation with a mentor.
3. The staffroom, where colleagues' attitudes and perceptions may be displayed.
4. At a meeting with learners' parents.
5. At an 'open advice' session for prospective students, where their aspir-ations and preconceptions regarding college life can be discerned.
6. Socially, when networking informally with other trainees.

Why it is helpful for mentors to underline the broad range of settings/circumstances in which critical incidents may be experienced is that there is some evidence that trainees may otherwise become somewhat fixated on the idea that they relate almost exclusively to confrontation in classrooms. In fact, a 'revelatory' observation from someone else's classroom (item 1 in the above list) can represent a critical incident – for example, some aspect of the practice which has been observed can lead to a fundamental rethinking of the trainee's own. Feedback given in an observation (item 2) may include a hugely important piece of much-needed confidence-building; this can happen when a trainee's self-perception of their performance to date has been extremely negative, overly self-critical – they have been undermining themselves. A mentor providing a degree of balance in this sort of situation is able, *critically*, to move things on by using words such as 'No, it wasn't anywhere near as bad as you think – actually you're being far too hard on yourself'.

References

Colley, H. (2003) *Mentoring for Social Inclusion: A Critical Approach to Nurturing Mentor Relationships.* London: RoutledgeFalmer.

Tripp, D. (1993) *Critical Incidents in Teaching.* London: Routledge.

Mentors' continuing professional development

Chapter objective:

- To draw attention to the potential for professional extension and advancement which a commitment to mentoring can realise.

In this short chapter I aim to focus on ways in which the effective, forward-looking mentor can build on his/her experiences by weaving them into and own personal 'professional projects' and plans to progress. Such 'projects' are being formally promoted in some colleges through the vehicle of the *personal development plans* (PDPs) which staff may use as the basis for their appraisals, and in connection with other institutional processes relating to human resources.

It seems wholly appropriate that involvement in the role of mentor is seen as a part of mentors' own continuing professional development. This is not only meant to refer to the positive benefits accruing to currently held teaching skills from observing and engaging in debate with trainees; it also relates to the ways in which mentors may actively exploit their experiences when seeking professional advancement, either within their present institution or elsewhere. In a number of respects, especially as the profile of mentoring continues to be raised in professional life, the kinds of skills mentors will have used are likely to be viewed as high-level ones, of value in responsible positions. They are, therefore, eminently *transferable* ones.

From certain perspectives, it may even emerge that the ability and willingness to engage in mentoring becomes an *essential*, rather than merely *desirable*, criterion for the majority of substantial posts in the college sector – in other words, one of the basic minimum requirements for appointment as a full-time, established teacher who has completed a post-qualifying year. Writing in the context of teachers/mentors delivering Skills for Life programmes, Jay Derrick, for example, airs the view that 'Mentoring must become a normal part of all experienced teachers' job roles' (Derrick 2004: 25).

(Interestingly, though, this writer adds the important observation that 'infra-structure needs to exist in all regions for training, supporting and quality assuring mentors' (ibid.). This would appear to further extend, regionally, the notion of an appropriate institutional architecture for mentoring proposed in Chapter 2.)

As a starting point for the creation of an *inventory* of skills and attributes to which attention can be drawn in applications being made for posts, it is, quite simply, perfectly legitimate to describe the degree of respect, and status, already accorded to an individual when they have been proposed or designated as a mentor. Although we can probably all think of instances where appointments to the mentor role have resulted from the 'no one else available' syndrome, these will be very rare. In general, selectors will almost certainly work on the assumption that mentors will have been given the responsibilities attached to the work for a mixture of the following reasons:

- relatively long service in an institution, or at the least a degree of 'loyalty' to it, and a history of positive interaction with colleagues and superiors;

- measurable skills in the area of self-organisation, and the management of course documentation;

- high-level classroom teaching skills, which are also, in a number of ways, susceptible to objective measures – for instance, gradings awarded in internal or external inspection exercises, or evaluative comments supplied by college learners;

- reliability, and perhaps the kind of willingness and flexibility attached to covering for absent colleagues – in a nutshell, a track record of taking on more than has, strictly speaking, been required in a post;

- less easily quantified – but vital – attributes (or 'dispositions') such as those FENTO/LLUK (2000) refer to as 'personal impact and presence', discussed earlier in connection with the observation of practical teaching.

Many of us are naturally reticent about making too many claims regarding our strengths, but the kinds of people skills and organisational skills routinely deployed by practising mentors are clearly very sought-after ones. This applies not only in respect of posts in the broad areas of education and training (includ-ing teacher training, of course) but also in related professional realms, if that is where our career aspirations happen to be leading us. It would, moreover, be feasible to supply evidence to substantiate the strengths to which one wishes to draw attention; for instance a record of the number of trainees successfully completing their programmes over a period of time, with a mentor's support.

Mentoring skills are, then, transferable ones, and in some ways are fairly clearly related to *management*, in its broadest sense – mentors have managed individual trainees' timetables (those on full-time, pre-service courses), effectively liaised with colleagues in compiling these, managed observations of classroom practice, structured debriefings following these, and taken on a 'troubleshooting' role when things have not all been as they should be. And *coaching*, an increasingly acknowledged and valued dimension of mentoring (or at least an adjunct to it), is another function that could be listed here. It is probably self-evident that these kinds of tasks are not at all dissimilar to those performed regularly by curriculum managers, and as such will be seen as constituting a useful preparation for such positions.

Furthermore, mentors will have written detailed formative and summative reports, been involved in target-setting and very possibly counselled trainees regarding career pathways in the PCET sector. All of these dimensions of being a mentor are well worth celebrating in applications, always being cautious not to dwell too much on the kinds of things referred to here at the expense of issues perhaps more strongly linked with specific sets of selection criteria. Good mentors have invested a great deal of their time, thought and energy to the induction and ongoing support of trainees, and it is entirely legitimate that such an investment might have somewhat longer-term professional rewards as well as those deriving from the day-to-day contact with trainees.

Some of the above ideas are worked into an interesting statement comprising 'recommendations for mentors' to be found in the collaborative *Mentoring Towards Excellence* (FENTO/AoC 2001: 8). This report describes the 'learning conversations about mentoring' held in 29 colleges in connection with this publication, which gave rise to the following list. Although some of the individual items read more like recommendations for college managers – or policy-makers – the list is notable for being an authoritative indication of recent thinking in at least some key PCET institutions.

Recommendations for mentors:

1. Mentoring should be developed and promoted as a supportive and developmental process.
2. The mentors should have job descriptions that clarify their role.
3. Mentoring and observation should apply to all teachers: full-time; part-time; supply and agency teachers.
4. Mentoring should be part of the management's commitment to improving quality and raising standards of teaching and learning.
5. Mentors should be best-practice practitioners.
6. Teaching observations should be used to identify 'grade 1' teachers who are strong role models to become mentors.

7. Mentors should be formally trained.

8. Mentors should be either paid for mentoring, or be given time to carry out the job.

9. Mentoring should be used to increase the sharing of good practice.

10. A mentor needs to be a successful practitioner with strong interpersonal skills.

If such a collation of points from the 'learning conversations' forming the research basis for the report were to gain a wide currency it could usefully serve to underscore the centrality of mentors' high standing in colleges, and thereby their suitability for further professional advancement.

Mentoring as a dimension of CPD

It has become commonplace that in any professional area there is now a need to demonstrate a readiness to continually refine and extend our skills. But in certain ways we may still have a somewhat blinkered view of what exactly can legitimately be described as 'professional development'. As Graham Guest has expressed it:

> It is easy to assume that CPD is just a matter of attending training courses off the job. This is certainly one aspect, but there are many more. CPD activities can include on-the-job training, open learning, short courses, conferences, seminars, workshops, self-study, preparing and making presentations and *being a coach or mentor.* (Guest 2004: 22, emphasis added)

From what we have seen of the demands of effective mentoring, and the range of skills which mentors must display, there is clearly much more professional development attached to the successful practice of the activity than would result from choosing, say, to remain 'purely' a classroom teacher (although this is, of course, not intended as a statement to in any way diminish the value of professional accomplishments in the classroom). Alongside this fact, it is indisputable that mentoring in the post-compulsory sector is to be accorded even greater value in the context of planned reforms to the training of new entrants to teaching within it. Therefore, there is evidently much to be gained by mentors who can navigate the various possibilities for celebrating what they have achieved – for themselves as well as for the trainees with whom they have worked.

One possible way in which mentoring activities might be documented might well be as part of a Personal Development Record (or Plan) (PDR/P). In fact, such a record 'may well soon become the norm, supplementing our on-line CVs and personal websites' (ibid.). The PDR could be organised in such a way as to highlight the *transferability* of the professional learning that has accrued from mentoring and, specifically, to indicate ways in which it has better equipped an individual for increased managerial responsibilities.

Not only mentoring itself, but also participating in mentoring-related activities is worthy of recognition as CPD. To link together two of the possibilities referred to by Guest (mentoring and preparing a presentation), it might be feasible to contribute to an organised event where the focus is best practice in mentoring; a number of practising mentors did so at a seminar organised at the writer's base institution in 2004, adding greatly to the credibility of the programme, it was felt.

However, if these kinds of considerations appear somewhat too instrumental, then it is probably necessary to re-attach this discussion to mentors' more immediate concerns, and focus on ways in which improvements to current practice can be sought. Some ideas of relevance to this end are presented below.

Improving the quality of one's mentoring

The ability to mentor effectively is susceptible to a range of quantitative and qualitative measures, some of these being:

- in an institution having in place transparent mechanisms for identifying staff to join a mentoring team, the very fact of having been selected for the role;
- successful completion by trainees of their programmes;
- evaluations completed by such trainees; and
- comments supplied, informally or formally, by withdrawing (perhaps even complaining) trainees.

The evolution of one's mentoring skills will be occurring as a result of using them regularly – the 'practice makes perfect' effect. But other positive effects can be derived from such activities as attending events with a 'sharing of best practice' focus and (even better) contributing to the design and delivery of these. Actively evaluating one's own practice is, however, to be commended even more highly. It is, then, worth giving some thought to how best to undertake this evaluation. Let us try to expand on the third point in the listing beginning this section.

'Group' evaluation exercises might be conducted where a number of trainees in one institution are asked to respond anonymously to written questions posed regarding the quality of mentoring they have received over a period. Each member of a team of mentors can examine and discuss the picture of mentoring which emerges, and make educated guesses concerning which evaluative comments (positive or negative) might apply to their own efforts.

This sort of strategy is liable to provide a useful overview, but is probably too blunt an instrument for most individual mentors' liking if they wish to acquire a greater degree of insight into how their own performance has been perceived.

The use of focus groups is worth considering, where trainees can discuss their experiences with mentors. Ideally, such a forum would be one in which the distorting effects of power relations are minimised, and one way of tackling this issue is simply by making sure that neither 'side' feels itself to be outnumbered. Aim, therefore, for as even a balance between mentors and trainees as can be engineered. Alternatively, where a focus group can be facilitated by a neutral third party, perhaps a college's staff development manager (although, admittedly, here 'neutrality' is questionable), this allows for a higher degree of comfort.

The above devices have obvious, quite severe, limitations when it comes to eliciting evaluations of an individual mentor's performance. To obtain such an evaluation will be contingent upon the trainees involved forfeiting their anonymity, and it must therefore be acknowledged to be a process which will only produce any reliable results where the mentor–trainee relationship has been an overwhelmingly positive one. It probably takes a relatively courageous trainee to offer honest feedback if this is negative. On the other hand, actually posing the difficult questions in the first place probably also calls for a measure of courage. As with so many other aspects of mentoring practice, the well-judged and skilful use of language in posing appropriate questions (in this specific context reassurance of 'no reprisals' being the obvious priority) will be a real asset to the mentor concerned.

Mentors' support for trainees is usually evaluated by training institutions, and more often than not there would be no obstacles presented to mentors actively seeking out how they have fared in such exercises. Again, however, training institutions would need a high degree of reassurance should seriously negative issues have been raised by a trainee – and on ethical grounds might in some instances not actually feel able to relay the contents of particular evaluations. Where such a response is encountered, it makes sense to ask for the assistance of the training provider in strongly encouraging a trainee to feel secure in raising even critical issues directly with their mentor or former mentor. It is virtually impossible to improve one's performance where the deficiencies are only being guessed at. But the summative evaluations, i.e. those carried out at the end of a trainee's programme, while they do not positively contribute to *ongoing* mentoring relationships, can profoundly influence the nature and effectiveness of future ones.

Accreditation for mentoring

This possibility has been touched on earlier, when dealing with some of the rewards of mentoring in Chapter 5. Here I merely reiterate that opportunities do exist at a number of universities to gain credit for the high-level, work-based professional learning for which mentoring provides evidence. Programmes are typically at Master's ('M') level, and successful completion of these is usually via a mix of portfolio assessment and extended writing (some of which will allow for a closer look at the kinds of theoretical models barely alluded to in Chapter 3). Oxford Brookes University's MA in Coaching and Mentoring Practice is of interest, as are programmes run at a number of other institutions including Middlesex University and Anglia Polytechnic University. One of the most positive aspects about such possibilities is that there exist options for APEL against relevant criteria.

College employers may be amenable to helping with the registration and other costs attached to these kinds of studies. The key to successful applications for such assistance seems to be being able to make a credible claim for the ways in which mentors see that their own practice, and teaching quality within an institution, can be enhanced by following one of the programmes. Clearly, however, the source of most relevant advice in this connection will be the senior individual within a college with staff development or human resources responsibilities.

Research and writing

At the outset I would need to acknowledge that a number of practising mentors will already possess a pedigree as published authors, especially in the realm of subject-specific texts. Here I will, however, focus on research and writing that might stem from the activity of mentoring itself. As well as seeking opportunities to document their own professional practice and to share it with others – perhaps those new to mentoring – with a view to possible career development, it is sometimes likely to be true that mentors' *academic* skills have yet further potential to be both refined and celebrated. Probably one of the most realistic, constructive and purposeful ways in which this might be accomplished is by engaging in research activity focusing on mentoring. A great deal of professional learning is actually taking place during mentoring relationships – sometimes the same kind of 'trial and error learning' which ordinary teaching might be said to entail.

Such learning can be viewed as leading to the kinds of 'really useful knowledge' it has become somewhat vogue-ish to speak of; the 'outcomes' of the learning are fairly immediately used to inform one's own professional practice and/or that of colleagues. In this sense we are almost on the verge of being able to claim that we are in the realm of action research. Such an approach is a highly appropriate one where 'the effects of a specific intervention are to be evaluated' (Cohen *et al.* 2000: 73). The 'intervention' in the present context would, of course, be the activity of mentoring.

A range of academic and professional journals would be receptive to individual or collaboratively written articles which focus on mentoring, including, for example:

- *Research in Post-Compulsory Education*
- *Journal of Vocational Education and Training*
- *Journal of Further and Higher Education*
- *Teacher Development*
- *International Journal of Mentoring and Coaching*

It is perhaps easy to be daunted by various aspects of writing for publication (not least by the prospect of trying to carve out in one's professional life sufficient time in which to get involved in the activity). However, many journals, including most of those above, have a strong *practitioner* focus, i.e. they are more concerned with case studies and action research projects (especially where improvements in quality can be evidenced as a result of the project) than with highly theoretical work. In other words, they often seek articles based on, and arising from, 'own professional practice' rather than ones largely or entirely divorced from this. It is true, though, that there is a kind of 'pecking order' of journals within the academic world, and the publications deemed to be most prestigious are often highly scholarly ones, aiming to be at the leading edge of empirical and theoretical studies, and these will certainly reject material they do not judge to be 'weighty' enough.

Beyond giving the obvious advice that it is therefore a good starting point to research the nature of the 'typical' article being accepted by any given journal, and its place in the status hierarchy of published academic writing, there are probably certain other key points (both positive and negative) to bear in mind:

- For the most strongly competed-for posts, being able to provide even a fairly brief publications record could be a distinctive feature of an application. Such an addition to an application could positively mark out a candidate.
- 'First-time' writers who are college-based might profitably seek out collaborative possibilities with trainers who have already published in relevant academic journals.
- Collaborative work with more immediate colleagues is also possible, bringing with it the potential to enhance the collegial ethos of an institution.
- The personal satisfaction of seeing one's work in print – and perhaps even on sale – is significant.
- A further, linked source of satisfaction lies in being involved with the dissemination to fellow mentors and others of best practice.

- When writing about matters such as the professional development of trainees, ethical issues need to be accorded special importance. This applies with special force to the area of trainee underperformance, when inadvertently allowing individuals to be identified could be viewed very seriously – not just ethically but legally.

- There are frustrations often in store because of the time lag between submission of work to a journal and its eventual publication. Commonly, journal articles will be reviewed by two independent referees before an intention to publish can be confirmed. Editorial and technical processes can add further delays – to the extent that a piece of writing can seem (to its author(s) more than its readers) to be quite dated by the time it appears.

- A strategy to avoid such frustrating experiences might be to seek internal opportunities to publish (e.g. in college newsletters/bulletins) and/or journals which are unrefereed.

- 'One thing might lead to another', as published work can stimulate the interest of academics, editors and other parties reading it, and this can bring about approaches to further develop ideas or to write on related themes.

Some 'horizon-scanning'

As I observed in introducing this guide, mentors are now at the very centre of current thinking with regard to initial teacher education. Consolidation of their role, and refinement of their approaches, will be witnessed over the coming years. I would anticipate that seeking a formal qualification will become far more of a majority pursuit among mentors, especially as almost certainly more universities and organisations will follow the lead of institutions such as Oxford Brookes University and the Chartered Institute of Professional Development in offering attractive routes to accreditation. Furthermore, we may increasingly find colleges placing successful mentoring far more prominently in their criteria for the award of 'advanced skills' status. As the observation of classroom teaching becomes an even more important dimension of various quality systems, so there will be an expanded requirement for *observer training* and mentors will surely have much to offer here.

At present there is a degree of hesitancy on the part of government (and certainly on the part of universities involved in ITE) to see even greater devolution of core training functions to employers/placements, but such a scenario is by no means being ruled out. Already in the school sector, mentors have a stronger, formalised involvement in judging trainees' eligibility for the award of their qualification to teach. Among some politicians and even educationists there is a lingering sentiment that schemes such as 'SCITT' (School-Centred Initial Teacher Training) offered the best – or at any rate least contaminated by 'barmy theory' – approach to preparing new entrants for the realities of classroom life. (The use of 'training' as opposed to 'education' in the designation of the schemes probably spoke volumes as regards their objectives.) Should such views come to hold sway, then the confidence and readiness of mentors to assume even greater responsibilities, within a significantly wider jurisdiction, will be all-important. So, too, will be the capacity of mentors to exercise their professional judgement even at the stage of selecting trainees with the potential to become effective teachers; a number of HEIs are, in fact, already involving practising mentors in this function, acknowledging the high value of their inputs to the process.

But the skills of mentoring are supremely transferable ones, to reiterate this key point, and merely being involved in such an activity as training others who will need to conduct a large number of teaching observations by no means sets a limit on the developmental opportunities which may be taken advantage of. Alongside this kind of role – and all the intrinsic satisfactions and rewards of mentoring which were summed up in Chapter 5 – there are other avenues to explore. Ever-widening participation in post-compulsory education is likely to trigger the development of more all-encompassing *student mentoring* schemes, and there will be a job to be done in contributing to the design of these. *Peer mentoring* – in particular where a key objective is the support and retention of specific cultural groups which the profession needs – will need strengthening. 'Even managers need mentors' and with the Centre for Excellence in Leadership currently expanding its role (CEL 2004) there are opportunities for mentors who also have – or will go on to have – management experience. On the other hand, for mentors opting, for whatever reason, to scale down their commitment to full-time college-based employment, there are almost always, it seems, ways open to acquire consultancy work in coaching and/or mentoring. More broadly, much training and development work, both within and outside the post-compulsory sector, will be far more confidently approached with a background in mentoring. While it would be to wildly overstate the case to say 'Be a mentor and anything is possible', the possibilities touched on here, surely, are not exhaustive.

Not everyone will find that they are drawn to mentoring as a professional activity, and not everyone will wish to continue with it on a long-term basis. It would be dishonest not to acknowledge that for some college-based practitioners the appeal of other endeavours – pastoral work with students, curriculum management or acquiring important responsibilities for resourcing and developing e-learning – will hold greater appeal. But for those choosing to further exploit the attributes and skills that led to their initial involvement in mentoring, I would say that these are exciting times.

References

CEL (2004) *Mentoring: Learning from Practice: Learning from Each Other*. London: Centre for Excellence in Leadership.

Cohen, L., Manion, L. and Morrison, M. (2000) *Research Methods in Education* (5th edn).

Derrick, J. (2004) 'Developing mentoring skills'. *Professional Development* (Basic Skills Bulletin), 1, October.

FENTO (2000) *Standards for Teaching and Supporting Learning in Further Education in England and Wales*. London: Further Education Training Organisation.

FENTO/AoC (2001) *Mentoring Towards Excellence*. London: Further Education National Training Organisation/Association of Colleges.

Guest, G. (2004) 'No longer an optional extra'. A*dults Learning*, 16(3), November, 22–4.

Proposed qualification routes for college teachers

This diagram demonstrates the qualification process for all teachers in the learning and skills sector.

- all are given initial assessment leading to an individual learning plan;
- subject-specific and generic mentors and coaches are provided;

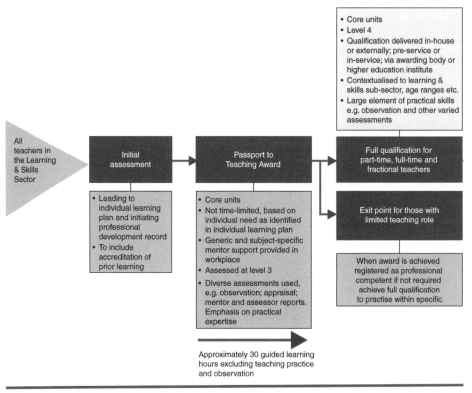

- Core units
- Level 4
- Qualification delivered in-house or externally; pre-service or in-service; via awarding body or higher education institute
- Contextualised to learning & skills sub-sector, age ranges etc.
- Large element of practical skills e.g. observation and other varied assessments

All teachers in the Learning & Skills Sector

Initial assessment

- Leading to individual learning plan and initiating professional development record
- To include accreditation of prior learning

Passport to Teaching Award

- Core units
- Not time-limited, based on individual need as identified in individual learning plan
- Generic and subject-specific mentor support provided in workplace
- Assessed at level 3
- Diverse assessments used, e.g. observation; appraisal; mentor and assessor reports. Emphasis on practical expertise

Full qualification for part-time, full-time and fractional teachers

Exit point for those with limited teaching role

When award is achieved registered as professional competent if not required achieve full qualification to practise within specific

Approximately 30 guided learning hours excluding teaching practice and observation

Up to 5 year registration

132

- all have to achieve the passport to teaching, except visiting speakers;
- those with only a limited teaching role may exit at this stage;
- part-time, full-time and fractional teachers, and anyone who wishes to, then starts the full qualification;
- teachers exit this stage with a full qualification, Qualified Teacher Learning & Skills, licence to practise . . . with a commitment to fulfil annual continuing professional development requirements;
- continuing professional development carries on throughout career.

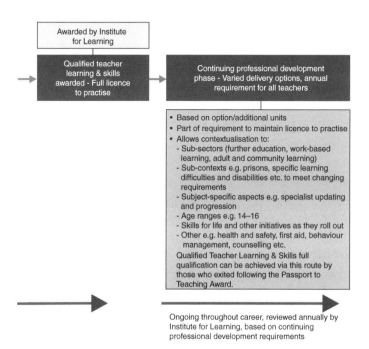

Ongoing throughout career, reviewed annually by Institute for Learning, based on continuing professional development requirements

The FENTO/LLUK Standards summarised

The Standards are currently organised under the following headings:

(a) assessing learners' needs;

(b) planning and preparing teaching and learning programmes for groups and individuals;

(c) developing and using a range of teaching and learning techniques;

(d) managing the learning process;

(e) providing learners with support;

(f) assessing the outcomes of learning and learners' achievement;

(g) reflecting upon and evaluating one's own performance and planning future practice;

(h) meeting professional requirements.

The standards consist of the following three main elements:

- professional knowledge and understanding;
- skills and attributes;
- key areas of teaching.

Professional knowledge and understanding

The knowledge and understanding required to perform effectively as an FE teacher are arranged in three categories:

- **domain-wide knowledge** applicable across all areas of professional practice;
- **generic knowledge** relating to each standard;
- **essential knowledge** relating to specific aspects of each standard.

The **domain-wide knowledge** is listed here. **Generic knowledge** appears in the introduction to each of the key areas of teaching. **Essential knowledge** is listed under each of the standards within key areas.

FE teachers and teaching teams should have domain-wide knowledge and critical understanding of:

(a)   the place of FE within the wider context;

(b)   the aims, objectives and policies of the organisation in which the teacher works;

(c)   professional knowledge in their own subject area;

(d)   learning theory, teaching approaches and methodologies;

(e)   social and cultural diversity and its effect on learning and on curriculum development and delivery;

(f)   the social, cultural and economic background of individual learners and the implications of this for learning and teaching;

(g)   ways of ensuring that linguistic diversity is valued and accommodated within programmes of learning and teaching;

(h)   current national and international initiatives and how they are interpreted within the strategic plan of the organisation;

(i)   current developments within their own specialist vocational or academic area of expertise and ways of keeping up to date with such developments;

(j)   the concept of inclusive learning;

(k)   learners' entitlements and issues related to the autonomy of the learner;

(l)   the broad range of learning needs including the needs of those with learning difficulties and/or disabilities, and the facilities and arrangements that are available to help meet these needs;

(m)   the characteristics of effective teaching;

(n)   how to measure effectiveness against a diverse range of quality indicators;

(o)   what constitutes best professional practice;

(p)   ways of analysing and using key information to inform teaching and learning;

(q)   effects of change on the FE sector and teachers' own practice;

(r)   methods of assessment;

(s)   information technology and how it can be used to extend and enhance learning;

(t)   ways of ensuring the currency and effectiveness of technical and educational competence and sources of professional development;

(u) models of curriculum development and how they can be applied in their own area of work;

(v) sources of funding and teachers' own contribution in accessing such funding.

Skills and attributes

In addition to the skills related to specific aspects of competence there are a number of generic personal skills, including interpersonal skills, and personal attributes, that should inform all aspects of teaching within FE.

Personal skills

Teachers and teaching teams should display the skills of:

- analysis;
- evaluation;
- monitoring and reviewing;
- planning and prioritising;
- setting objectives;
- managing time;
- research and study;
- critical self-reflection;
- identifying, interpreting and applying specific knowledge to practice;
- problem-solving;
- creativity;
- decision-making;
- handling conflict;
- establishing effective working relationships;
- communicating effectively with groups and individuals with specific reference to:

    preparing effective written materials
    listening and questioning skills
    explaining ideas clearly
    providing constructive feedback
    contributing to group discussions
    working collaboratively with others
    networking

interviewing
negotiating
managing themselves
managing change
presenting and delivering information.

Personal attributes

Teachers and teaching teams should possess and display:

- personal impact and presence;
- enthusiasm;
- self-confidence;
- energy and persistence;
- reliability;
- intellectual rigour;
- integrity;
- appreciation of FE values and ethics;
- commitment to education and to learners' progress and achievement;
- readiness to adapt to changing circumstances and new ideas;
- realism;
- openness and responsiveness to others;
- acceptance of differing learning needs, expectations and styles;
- empathy, rapport and respect for learners and colleagues;
- assertiveness.

Key areas of teaching

Standards have been developed to cover all the major areas of activity:

(a) Assessing learners' needs.
(b) Planning and preparing teaching and learning programmes for groups and individuals.
(c) Developing and using a range of teaching and learning techniques.
(d) Managing the learning process.
(e) Providing learners with support.
(f) Assessing the outcomes of learning and learners' achievements.

(g) Reflecting upon and evaluating one's own performance and planning future practice.

In addition to these, there is an underpinning competence of meeting professional requirements which supports and informs all other processes. This has been expressed as a set of values and principles, separate from the other statements of competence but implicit in all the standards.

(h) Meeting professional requirements.

Summary of the key areas of teaching

(a) **Assessing learners' needs.** This involves being able to:

- identify and plan for the needs of potential learners;
- make an initial assessment of learners' needs.

(b) **Planning and preparing teaching and learning programmes for groups and individuals.** This involves being able to:

- identify the required outcomes of the learning programme;
- identify appropriate teaching and learning techniques;
- enhance access to and participation in learning programmes.

(c) **Developing and using a range of teaching and learning techniques.** This involves being able to:

- promote and encourage individual learning;
- facilitate learning in groups;
- facilitate learning through experience.

(d) **Managing the learning process.** This involves being able to:

- establish and maintain an effective learning environment;
- plan and structure learning activities;
- communicate effectively with learners;
- review the learning process with learners;
- select and develop resources to support learning;
- establish and maintain effective working relationships;
- contribute to the organisation's quality-assurance system.

(e) **Providing learners with support.** This involves being able to:

- induct learners into the organisation;
- provide effective learning support;
- ensure access to guidance opportunities for learners;
- provide personal support to learners.

(f) **Assessing the outcomes of learning and learners' achievements.** This involves being able to:

- use appropriate assessment methods to measure learning and achievement;
- make use of assessment information.

(g) **Reflecting upon and evaluating one's own performance and planning future practice.** This involves being able to:

- evaluate one's own practice;
- plan for future practice;
- engage in continuing professional development.

(h) **Meeting professional requirements.** This competence underpins all other competences. It involves being able to:

- work within a professional value base;
- conform to agreed codes of professional practice.

Further reading

Journals

Mentoring increasingly features in relevant academic journals, some of which are named in the chapter on mentors' continuing professional development (Chapter 8). Certain journals, including *Mentoring and Tutoring, Partnership in Learning*, focus specifically on issues of special relevance to mentors. Recent articles carried in this include:

'Mentoring online about mentoring: possibilities and practice' (Catherine Sinclair); 'Mentoring in black and white: the intricacies of cross-cultural mentoring' (Juanita Johnson-Bailey and Ronald M. Cervero).

A free on-line sample copy of *Mentoring and Tutoring* can be obtained by visiting: www.tandf.co.uk/journals/onlinesamples.asp

Websites

This is an extremely selective listing. It is especially hard to provide any kind of adequate, informative overview of the numerous subject-specific websites which have been designed by interested professionals and subject associations.

Centre for Excellence in Leadership: http://www.centreforexcllence.org.uk

This site focuses on the ways in which mentoring and coaching are being used to enhance the quality of *leadership* in the learning and skills sector. It incorporates material on the kinds of mentoring models seen by CEL as those most appropriate for its specific brief. It also outlines its important connection with the Black Leadership Initiative mentoring scheme, and provides guidance on how managers interested in entering a mentoring relationship can arrange for the services of one of CEL's network of mentors.

Department for Education and Skills: http://www.dfes.gov.uk

This is probably the most useful single site for updates on policy, consultations in progress and emerging changes in the legislative framework in which initial teacher education is offered.

Education Arena: http://www.educationarena.com

This site attempts 'to provide information on all matters relating to education and educational research in one central location' and carries notices of forth-coming conferences, etc. Sample articles, sometimes of possible interest to mentors, are available on-line.

European Mentoring and Coaching Council: http://www.emccouncil.org

A useful site for mentors interested in looking at more international perspec-tives, although, of course, material from the UK does feature. Accessing the emcc's site allows access to the on-line *International Journal of Mentoring and Coaching*. This carries a range of interesting case studies and often contains articles exploring more fully some of the theoretical perspectives touched on in this guide.

Further Education National Training Organisation: http://.www.fento.org.uk

The body currently responsible for specifying the occupational standards which must be covered during a trainee's course.

Higher Education Academy: http://www.hea.org.uk

Launched in 2004, the successor body to the Institute for Learning and Teaching in Higher Education (ILTHE) publicises its developmental activities through this site. Its relevance to PCET is best illustrated in *Equipping Our Teachers for the Future*: 'There may . . . be opportunities to work with the HE Academy, encouraging more joint CPD programmes between further education colleges and HEIs involved in the delivery of Foundation Degree programmes' (DfES 2004: 12). The HEA is paying real attention to the learning and teaching challenges presented by the accelerating diversification and massification of HE; current best practice in responding to such challenges can be gleaned from the site, and will be of interest.

Institute of Continuing Professional Development: http://.cpdinstitute.org

This site offers useful cross-professional perspectives on CPD, including some from education.

Institute for Learning: http://.www.ifl.org

The relatively new professional body for teachers in the post-compulsory sector uses its website to provide updates both on emerging government policies for the sector and on best practice within it.

Learning and Skills Development Agency: http://.www.LSDA.org.uk

Of value as a site for various reasons, including its updates on research in progress in colleges, best practice reports, and analysis of the success of policy initiatives.

Office for Standards in Education: http://.www.ofsted.gov.uk

An essential site for providing a picture of what is being seen across the PCET sector in the course of the Inspection process. Details of the quality of teacher training being provided at recently inspected institutions is also available, as OfSTED's remit includes this area.

TeacherNet: http://.www.teachernet.gov.uk

A DfES website which aims to promote continuing professional development, and strategies for the improvement of learning and teaching. Although strongly schools-focused, material of relevance and interest to practitioners in PCET is to be found.

Teacher Training Agency (TTA): http://.www.tta.gov.uk

The TTA is the body overseeing and setting standards for training for teaching in the schools sector. Although the possibility of formalising links between the TTA and the various bodies involved in training for PCET was much discussed at one point, it has now been clearly ruled out (DfES 2004: 6–7). However, this website provides some interesting insights into the current concerns and pre-occupations of school-focused training – which may be seen as of strong relevance within the context of challenges being posed by the emerging 14–19 curriculum.

Teaching Times: http://.www.teachingtimes.co.uk

Another useful website for providing 'snapshots' of educational developments and debates. Primarily schools-focused, but has also recently included items such as one describing the staff recruitment problems being faced by colleges, locating this issue within the debate over salary discrepancies between college teachers and their counterparts in schools. News items such as any outstanding inspection results being achieved by colleges are also sometimes featured.

Times Educational Supplement: http://.tesfefocus.co.uk

A good website for comment and analysis relating specifically to the college sector – a straightforward way for practitioners to keep abreast of current concerns, learn about developments at particular institutions, and contribute to important debates.

Reference

DfES (2004) *Equipping Our Teachers for the Future: Reforming Initial Teacher Training for the Learning and Skills Sector.* Nottingham: Department for Education and Skills.

Index

David Fulton Publishers

In at the Deep End
A Survival Guide for Teachers in Post-Compulsory Education

Jim Crawley

Working in post-compulsory education can sometimes feel like being *'in at the deep end'*: teaching a highly diverse and sometimes challenging student group, trying to manage a rapidly changing and developing curriculum, a generally increasing workload and working with a level of bureaucracy that could defeat the faint-hearted – and that just takes care of Monday and Tuesday! The difference between sinking and swimming can be a small one . . .

   This positive and practical 'survival' guide will help you to effectively manage these varied demands by offering friendly, professional advice and support on:

- Meeting the initial challenges, working positively with your students, supporting key skills and basic skills
- Accessing support, working with colleagues and managing conflict
- Handling challenging behaviour, making positive use of ICT and teaching your specialist subject
- Managing inspections, developing as a leader and becoming a reflective professional

Lively and engaging, this book will help all new teachers overcome everyday problems and pressures to keep their *'heads above water'* and become efficient, skilled professionals in the post-compulsory workplace.

Jim Crawley is Head of Lifelong Learning at Bath Spa University

£12.99 • Paperback • 192 pp • 1-84312-253-7 • May 2005

Leadership in Post-Compulsory Education
Inspiring Leaders of the Future

Jill Jameson

Leadership of different kinds exists at many levels in the post-compulsory sector – from principals to programme leaders, administrative staff and even caretakers. Based on case studies of current leaders in post-compulsory education, this unique book explores a number of leadership models and styles in order to provide inspiration and guidance for the next wave of potential leaders.

- Captures authentic 'voices of the leaders'
- Includes examples from further, adult, community and prison education
- Covers all type of leadership: charismatic leaders, academic leaders, spiritual leaders, women leaders, ethnic leaders, business leaders

Presenting a wide and holistic view of leadership at a variety of levels, this book is relevant for all potential and current leaders in post-compulsory education. By encouraging readers to review and reflect on the models described, the book will inspire leaders of the future to develop their own leadership styles and visions.

Jill Jameson is a Principal Lecturer in Lifelong Learning, Education and Training at the University of Greenwich.

£12.99 • Paperback • 150pp • 1-84312-339-8 • October 2005